THIS BOOK SHOULD BE RETURNED ON OR BEFORE THE LATEST
DATE SHOWN TO THE LIBRARY FROM WHICH IT WAS BORROWED

AUTHOR

CLASS

TITLE

Lancashire
County
Council

THE LANCASHIRE LIBRARY.
Library Headquarters,
143, Corporation St.,
PRESTON PRI 2TB.

D0544654

THE CHAIRMAN

A Play

by

PHILIP MACKIE

SAMUEL FRENCH

LONDON
NEW YORK TORONTO SYDNEY HOLLYWOOD

© 1976 BY PHILIP MACKIE

This play is fully protected under the copyright laws of the British Commonwealth of Nations, the United States of America, and all countries of the Berne and Universal Copyright Conventions.

All rights are strictly reserved.

It is an infringement of the copyright to give any public performance or reading of this play either in its entirety or in the form of excerpts without the prior consent of the copyright owners. No part of this publication may be transmitted, stored in a retrieval system, or reproduced in any form or by any means, electronic, mechanical, photocopying, manuscript, typescript, recording, or otherwise, without the prior permission of the copyright owners.

SAMUEL FRENCH LTD, 26 SOUTHAMPTON STREET, STRAND, LONDON WC2E 7JE, or their authorized agents, issue licences to amateurs to give performances of this play on payment of a fee. **The fee must be paid and the licence obtained before a performance is given.**

Licences are issued subject to the understanding that it shall be made clear in all advertising matter that the audience will witness an amateur performance; and that the names of the authors of the plays shall be included on all announcements and on all programmes.

The royalty fee indicated below is subject to contract and subject to variation at the sole discretion of Samuel French Ltd.

The publication of this play must not be taken to imply that it is necessarily available for performance by amateurs or professionals, either in the British Isles or overseas. Amateurs intending production must, in their own interests, make application to Samuel French Ltd or their authorized agents, for consent before starting rehearsals or booking a theatre or hall.

Basic fee for each and every
performance by amateurs   Code M
in the British Isles

In theatres or halls seating 600 or more the fee will be subject to negotiation.

In territories overseas the fee quoted above may not apply. Application must be made to our local authorized agents, or if there is no such agent, to Samuel French Ltd, London.

Applications to perform the play by professionals should be made to CLIVE GOODWIN ASSOCIATES, 79 Cromwell Road, London SW7 5BN.

ISBN 0 573 11068 9

4 6 5 2 2 5 9 9 3

MADE AND PRINTED IN GREAT BRITAIN BY
LATIMER TREND & COMPANY LTD PLYMOUTH
MADE IN ENGLAND

THE CHAIRMAN

First presented by Hazel Vincent Wallace at the Thorndike Theatre, Leatherhead, and subsequently by Michael White at the Globe Theatre, London, on May 10th, 1976, with the following cast of characters:

David Pulman	Tony Britton
Richard Pershore	David Firth
Peter Frame	Peter Blythe
Rodney Spurling	Barrie Cookson
Ken Grist	Reginald Marsh
Doctor Ducker	Michael Malnick
Veronica	Sarah Atkinson
Eve	Jill Melford

The Play directed by Gareth Davies
Setting by Stuart M Stanley

ACT I   Now
ACT II   Later

Time—the present

ACT I

SCENE 1

The firm of Greatrick Limited. Daytime

Most of the stage is taken up by David Pulman's office. He is the Director of Public Relations. Greatrick Limited, is a large and important firm, so his office is large and important. He sits behind a splendid desk (this is used on occasion as a conference table). The office has a door each side. One is a private door leading to the corridor. The other, the normal way in and out, leads to a much smaller office—a kind of ante-room to his. This is Veronica's office. Veronica is his secretary, and this office is where she guards his privacy and maintains his importance. Above the office, on a rostrum, a corridor stretches from one side of the stage to the other, leading off in either direction. On each side a short flight of stairs leads to Veronica's office and the private door to Pulman's office. At the head of each flight is a lift with automatic sliding doors. At the back of Veronica's office, by the side of the stairs, is a shelf with a small, practical tea and coffee vending machine. See plan of set on p. 75

As the CURTAIN *rises, Peter Frame and Richard Pershore come out of the lift* L *and along the corridor—except that Frame has a disconcerting habit of stopping suddenly to make a point. Veronica is sitting at her desk. Ken Grist is sitting in Pulman's office*

Frame Of course David entirely agrees, he totally takes my point, you'll see for yourself, he's marvellous at taking points, that everyone in the Department must subscribe, sincerely subscribe, to the same basic theory of public relations, but bringing to it in practice different qualities of mind, as I felt you had a quality, a new quality, which would help us to do what we must do to each other all the time . . . cross-pollinate.

Richard Yes . . .

Frame You agree?

Richard Yes indeed.

Frame I felt at the interview there was a marvellous directness about your responses—sometimes we tend to theorize too long, one so easily can, terrible temptation to over-elaborate, we need a fresh eye, a child's eye, a voice to call us back to simplicity, we need someone who can stand there and say: "But he's got no clothes on."

Richard Yes.

Frame You might be the person to say it.

Richard Right.

Frame So glad you met David the other day, I know it was brief but terribly lucky, of course we discussed you at length, there was no question, marvellous at delegation while retaining absolute control, you'll see, velvet hand as if it weren't there, and perpetually killing two birds with one stone and they don't even know they've been killed. Genius.

They go down the stairs into Veronica's office. Veronica is brilliantly handling two telephones at once, with dazzling charm, and some to spare for the intruders

Veronica (*on one phone*) Hullo? . . . Oh, would you hold on a moment, Henry, my other phone's going. . . . (*On the other phone*) Hullo? . . . Oh, Mr Cutts, did you want David? I'm afraid he's all tied up at the moment, a thing for the Chairman, I simply daren't disturb him. . . . Yes. Yes, of course. The moment he's free. Good-bye, Mr Cutts. . . . Yes, I will. 'Bye. (*She hangs up. To Frame and Peter*) Hullo. So sorry. Do sit down. (*On the other phone*) Henry, I'm afraid Mr Pulman's tied up, all I can do is put your name on the list, and it's a terribly long list. . . . Yes. Yes, you do that. See you. 'Bye. (*She hangs up*) Good morning, Peter.

Frame Veronica, can I introduce . . .
Veronica Mr Pershore, how d'you do?
Richard How d'you . . .
Veronica (*to Frame*) You had an appointment with David?
Frame Yes, he wanted to . . .
Veronica I'm terribly sorry.
Frame All tied up?
Veronica Hand and foot. The Chairman.
Frame Ah, well.
Veronica (*lifting a piece of paper*) But I do have a message for you.
Frame (*holding out his hand for it*) Can I . . .?
Veronica In shorthand?
Frame No.
Veronica (*reading*) "Be a good chap and hand him over to Ken Grist."
Frame (*sulkily*) Well, I . . .
Veronica (*reading*) "It would be a big help for today. Think of tomorrow. David."
Frame (*bright again*) Ah. Yes. Yes, of course.
Veronica He's in there.
Frame David?
Veronica Ken Grist. Waiting to see David. But David's not there.
Frame Tell him I absolutely understand. Tell him I think he's absolutely right. (*He is making for Pulman's office*)
Veronica 'Bye.
Richard (*responding with smile for smile*) 'Bye.

Frame knocks on the door, and enters Pulman's office. Ken Grist is there. He is about fifty, with the sad-funny face of an unsuccessful comedian. Frame does not care for him

Frame Oh, hullo! I heard you were here!
Grist (*rising*) Just waiting to have a word with the Great White Chief, when he comes free from his multifarious duties!
Frame Yes, well, sorry to interrupt you . . .

Grist What am I here for? Middle name coitus—and don't ask me what that means, I'm not going to tell you!

Frame But David did ask me to ask you if you could possibly spare the time——

Grist My time is your time, Peter!

Frame (*bringing Richard in*) —to indoctrinate—Richard Pershore . . .

Grist (*coming forward*) Ah-ha! The new boy, if I am not mistaken?

Richard That's right, sir.

Frame Mr Grist is our——

Grist Ken! Ken to everyone in this building! You ought to know that by now, Peter!

Frame —our Assistant Director of Public Relations . . .

Grist Remind me to tell you the one about the typist who left the "L" out. And I don't mean out of Relations.

Frame Ken, if you would be so good as to . . .

Grist Leave him to me, Peter! Thirty-eight years with the firm, if I can't, who can—except the Chairman, and he's got better things to do . . . (*To Richard*) Richard?

Richard Yes.

Grist Dick—welcome to Greatrick!

Richard Thank you, sir.

Grist Ken! I told you, Ken!

Richard Sorry, Ken.

Frame Well, if you'll excuse me . . . (*He slips out quickly to Veronica's office. There he makes a face expressive of relief at getting away*)

Veronica smiles sympathetically

Frame goes up to the corridor and off R

Grist First thing you've got to learn about Greatrick. This is a democratic organization. Ken. Dick. Peter. Everyone in the firm, from highest to lowest. Christian names all the way up and down.

Richard Yes, I see.

Grist It helps. It really helps.

Richard I'm sure it does.

Grist I think I still have a copy of the original memo sent round by the Chairman, I used to keep his memos, you know. Wonderful stuff. Churchillian.

Richard Oh yes?

Grist (*quoting*) "This is a democratic organization. You are not working for bosses. You are working for Greatrick. So there are no Misters or Masters in this firm. Everyone is plain Tom, Dick or Harry. Signed, the Chairman." . . . Nineteen forty-six that was. Not bad for a memory?

Richard Congratulations.

Grist Of course, it did wonders for morale. At that time, people just back from the war, Labour Government. It was good thinking.

Richard Churchillian.

Grist And you know he even let us count our war service. A half year

for every year away; and when it was all over everyone was taken
back at the same rate of pay as nineteen thirty-nine.

Richard Wonderful.

Grist You're working for a very generous organization, Dick. (*He looks
at his watch*) Speaking of which, it's about time for a drop of the in-
nocent stimulant. You like some?

Richard What?

Grist Unfortunately they don't bring it round any more. Not like in the
good old days. Good old days, but the coffee wasn't so hot. (*He sings,
to the tune of "Beer, Glorious Beer"*)
    Coffee, coffee, glorious coffee,
    Our girls can't make it for toffee,
    Cold as snow it is,
    Like H-two-o it is . . .
We used to have a Christmas concert every year. I used to make up
songs for it. Parodies. That sort of thing.

Richard That was very good.

Grist Sadly fallen into disuse since we expanded and diversified, and took
over, and merged. It was Soft Drinks, then. Just Soft Drinks. Nothing
else. (*Joking*) Hard drinks once a year, at the concert.

Richard It sounds fun.

Grist It was All Fools' Night. I remember the Chairman saying that to
me. "Ken," he said, "it's All Fools' Night. You have my permission to
say what you please. For this one night." And by golly we did.

Richard I bet you did.

Grist We made jokes about him—the Chairman. And he didn't turn a
hair. Not a single hair.

Richard Really?

Grist I came up through Soft Drinks, you see. Trainee, then Assistant,
then Salesman, then Deputy Area Manager, then Area Manager, then
the accolade, the transfer to Headquarters. (*He goes into Veronica's
office*) Hullo, Veronica! Just coming out for a cup of coffee!

Richard follows Grist

Veronica Right, Ken!

Grist Going to give young Dick here some instruction in the essential
art of working the machine!

Veronica (*smiling indomitably*) That's what he needs, Ken!

Grist It's always the same in Greatrick! It's no good pushing! And it's
no good pulling! You just put your tuppence in! And you wait for the
result!

Veronica It's more than tuppence now, Ken!

Veronica takes a file and exits upstairs R

Grist But the principle is the same! Come on, young Dick!

Grist goes to the vending machine, with coins

Now then, young Dick, what's it to be? With sugar or without? Black, white of khaki? We have all the varieties!

Richard Khaki, please. Without.

Grist One with, one without. That's life, isn't it?

Richard Yes.

Grist That's what Edna used to say. She was one of the tea girls. Poor old Edna. Wonder where she's gone. Great character, she was. (*He is putting coins into the vending machine, to get coffee in paper cups*)

Richard Was she?

Grist Everyone here. All great characters. Always ready for a laugh.

Richard Great.

Grist I put up a slogan to the Chairman once. "Think Great—think Greatrick!"

Richard Brilliant.

Grist I thought it hit a few nails on the head.

Richard Yes indeed.

Grist It nearly got through. Very nearly. (*He gives coffee to Richard*)

Richard Thank you. But I don't think you should pay for me . . .

Grist Take your chances while you can, Dick! It may never happen again!

Richard It's very kind of you.

Grist Behave as if nothing had happened. As the bishop said to the actress. And as he also said, now we're at the coffee stage, let's get down to business. You want to know how to get on in Greatrick?

Richard I'd be grateful for any advice.

Grist Good lad. Sit you down there.

He sits Richard on a stool below Veronica's desk

Right. Lesson number one. Keep your nose clean—and your desk as clean as your nose is.

Richard Ah.

Grist Lesson number two—now that you've got a drop of that fluid in-inside you, you won't mind if I say something personal.

Richard Oh?

Grist Don't take a wrong meaning from it, you weren't to know, nobody told you. But for your own good.

Richard I won't take a wrong meaning.

Grist Good lad. The Chairman doesn't like suede shoes.

Richard (*whose feet are guilty*) Ah.

Grist He said to me once—speaking of someone else, of course—"Ken— it's not that I'm against suede shoes myself—it's just that they're not Greatrick."

Richard Thank you for telling me.

Grist Black leather shoes. Polished so you can see your face in them. That's Greatrick.

Richard D'you think I ought to . . . ?

Grist Word from the wise, old son. Nip out at lunchtime and buy a pair. Like mine. (*He admires his own shoes*)

Richard Yes, I will.

Grist (*still admiring his own shoes*) Shall I ever forget the first time I wore these ones. Pure accident—I just happened to have bought them—but what a day that was. Message waiting when I got in—I went up to see him, in fear and trembling, of course, in case I'd committed some crime against holy writ. No. "Ken, I'm going to take you out of Soft Drinks. You've done a great job there. It's time you moved on. As this whole company is moving on, Ken. Not just Soft Drinks any longer. Toys, Publishing, who knows what next. Big. So we're going to do like the big companies do. We're going to have a Public Relations Department. Don't ask me why—they tell me we ought to have one so we're having one." Of course he was joking. "They tell me." No-one ever told him anything. Then he said, "New people coming in. Public Relations experts. But they've got one thing lacking. They don't know Greatrick. They don't know our ways. Ken, I'm putting you in there as Assistant Director of the Department. To teach them our ways."

Richard Yes, that must have been a great day for you.

Grist Certainly was! Make the most of it, Dick! Last of the young ones I'll teach our ways!

Richard You mean you're—leaving . . .?

Rodney Spurling comes along the corridor towards them. He is a quiet careworn man of forty-five

Grist Hail, Rodney!

Richard rises

Spurling Hullo, Ken.

Grist Rodney, I want you to meet young Dick Pershore, who joined Greatrick today.

Spurling How d'you do?

Grist Dick, this is Rodney Spurling, Press Officer Extraordinary.

Richard How d'you do?

Grist And I mean that! The only honest press man in the business! You're coming tonight, Rodney?

Spurling Oh, the . . .?

Grist Six o'clock, David's office.

Spurling Yes. See you then. Excuse me . . .

With a nod, Spurling fades away up the stairs L

Grist and Richard go up and towards the lift R

Grist I wonder if you'd like to come, Dick.

Richard To . . .?

Grist Six o'clock tonight. Just a few of the old colleagues, you know. Just a few drinks, to say "Hail and farewell, so long, be seeing you". You'd be very welcome.

Richard It's very nice of you, but . . .

Grist And the Chairman. The Chairman's promised to come. I had a word with his secretary this morning. He's promised to look in. He wouldn't miss a thing like that. Thirty-eight years with the firm I've been. I mean, you've got to acknowledge thirty-eight years. I mean, he couldn't possibly miss it. Not with that length of service.

Grist and Richard exit by the lift L

The Lights fade to a Black-out

SCENE 2

Veronica, in her office, is getting bottles of gin and whisky out of a carton, and carrying them into Pulman's office. There, she arranges bottles and glasses on the drinks cabinet. Grist and Richard come along the corridor towards her office

Grist (*consulting his watch*) See what the time is?
Richard About six?

Veronica prepares the drinks, on a tray

Grist Six o'clock, on the absolute dot. There's a pointer for you, Dick. You notice what time we went out to lunch?
Richard One o'clock?
Grist One o'clock on the dot. And you notice what time we walked back in?
Richard Two o'clock?
Grist On the literal dot.
Richard Yes, I see.
Grist Of course, in the old days he used to do it more often.
Richard The Chairman?
Grist Ring up at two minutes to one, ring up at one minute past two. "Could I speak to So-and-so, please?" "I'm sorry, he's not back from lunch yet." "Oh, isn't he? This is the Chairman speaking. Ask him to be so good as to come and see me the moment he's back." And of course, if he smelt alcohol on their breath—the chopper. Two half-pints and a Polo. I've been sticking to that for thirty-eight years.
Richard But the drinks tonight . . . ?

Veronica returns to her office for more bottles

Grist That's different. After office hours. On duty on duty, off duty off duty.
Richard Ah, yes.
Grist Besides, a man with my length of service . . .

They enter Veronica's office. She has bottles in her arms

What ho, that's what I like to see!
Veronica Hullo, Ken. (*To Richard*) Hullo.
Richard Let me help you with those.

Veronica Thank you.
Richard (*taking the bottles*) Where do I . . . ?
Veronica On the table in there.
Richard Right. (*He goes into Pulman's office*)
Grist Well, Veronica! Big night tonight!
Veronica Yes, I suppose it must be, for you.
Grist I mean with the Chairman coming.
Veronica Oh, really?
Grist He's promised to look in. I spoke to Miss Honeywell this morning.
Veronica Oh, yes?
Grist Farewell party after thirty-eight years, he couldn't miss that, could he?
Veronica I suppose not.

Richard comes back

Richard Any more I can do?
Veronica Yes, these tonic bottles and ginger ales in that cupboard . . .
Richard Sure. (*He helps*)
Grist Well, I think I'd be quite in order if I commenced the proceedings with a modicum of gin!

Veronica exits L. *Rodney Spurling comes in down the* R *stairs*

Grist Hail, Rodney!
Spurling Hullo, Ken.

Grist takes Spurling to the main office

Grist And welcome! You've saved me from the horrible vice of solitary drinking! What you having? I think there's everything—if you don't see what you want, I'll run out and buy it for you!
Spurling Just a bitter lemon, please, Ken.
Grist What, you setting a bad example to the young 'uns? I don't know what Dick'll think of you.
Spurling My stomach's not been so good . . .

Eve comes in downstairs through Veronica's office. She is a handsome woman in her late thirties

Grist (*to Spurling*) Here you are, if you insist.
Spurling Cheers, Ken. And congratulations.
Grist On what?
Spurling Leaving.
Grist Well, I don't know about that . . .
Eve Do I hear the sound of revelry by night?

Eve enters Pulman's office, and flings her arms wide to embrace Grist dramatically

Ken! Blessed above all men! He who has attained the summit—the
Everest—of human happiness! Who is leaving Greatrick!

Grist Hold on, Eve. Got to keep tidy for special guests.

Eve Who so special as us?

Grist Well, you never know who might turn up. Dick, this is our glamorous
magazine editress. Eve, can I introduce our newest recruit, Dick Pershore?

Eve Hullo.

Grist He joined us this morning.

Frame enters down the R stairs

Eve A day already? "Shades of the prison-house begin to close Upon the
growing boy ..."

Richard Can I pour you a drink?

Eve With a generous hand.

Grist sees Peter Frame coming in

Grist Come along, Peter! You're a drink behind everybody else! You'll
have to drink fast to catch up! What'll it be?

Frame The merest touch of vodka, please.

Grist And don't forget, any help you want on the agenda, just let me
know.

Frame The what?

Grist The agenda. For the Friday morning conference.

Frame Oh.

Grist Word from the wise. The Chairman's very hot on agendas.

Frame Oh yes?

Grist I should know, things I've been through with him. Minutes, matters
arising, any other business. If you want me to give you a hand ...

Frame No thanks. (*He takes the drink*) Thanks.

Grist I remember once, Dick, don't go, 'cos this'll interest you, old Soft
Drinks days, new chap called Fairfield taking the minutes. The Chairman read them and rang me up. "Ken! The man who wrote these! Send
him to Outer Mongolia or somewhere!" "Right, sir. May I ask why,
sir?" "Minutes? They're more like hours!"

Grist laughs. Nobody else does

Frame Yes, that's the Chairman.

Grist Bit clean, I admit. But it made me laugh, at the time. "Minutes?
They're more like hours!" (*He laughs again*)

Veronica enters her own office

Frame (*meaninglessly*) Yes.

Grist Well, let's get on with the business of this meeting! (*He pours more
drinks*)

Richard goes to Veronica's office

Richard Ouf!

Veronica Do you find it totally appalling?

Richard Frightening.

Veronica No, not frightening. Just appalling.

Richard I've had him all day long.

Veronica Poor you.

Richard Teaching me Greatrick's ways.

Veronica Why did you join?

Richard I'm twenty-eight.

Veronica Is that a reason?

Richard I'm normal. Hyper-normal. I fell in love.

Veronica And?

Richard And I thought, I must stop mucking about. Steady job. Security. Where's security? In the big organization. Whatever it's called. They're all the same. Whether they make oil, or chemicals, or copying machines. They've all got pension schemes. That's what matters. So who's advertising the vacancy?

Veronica You got the job. Do you still want it?

Richard I think nobody should work for anybody else.

Veronica Idle dream.

Richard No, the point is "for anybody else". May I use your phone?

Veronica You dial nine for an outside line.

Richard If it's all right to make a private call.

Veronica I didn't hear what you said. (*She turns and goes into Pulman's office*)

Richard I said . . . (*He realizes what she meant*) Sorry . . . (*He starts to dial*)

Grist (*in Pulman's office*) Well now . . .

Eve Are you going to make a speech?

Grist (*to Eve*) No, no, there's not going to be any speeches! At least, not till You-know-who comes through that door!

Eve I don't know who. Who?

Grist You don't know who?

Eve Should I?

Grist You don't know who comes through the door and catches you with orange peel on the floor, electric razor in your hand, fly buttons undone? When you thought he was in Bermuda?

Eve Don't wear fly buttons. I give up. Who?

Grist This was where they used to chant at the Christmas concert: "Our respected—our revered—our beloved—Chairman!"

Eve Oh, him. Is he coming?

Grist Eve, let me tell you what Miss Honeywell said this morning—in confidence . . . (*He takes her aside*)

Richard (*on the phone*) Jenny? . . . Richard. Jenny, I'm terribly sorry, I'm afraid I'm going to be late. There's this thing going on, I'm afraid I can't get away. . . . It's a party, a leaving party, there's this man, I can't tell you about him now, but he's leaving. . . . Darling, I am stone cold sober! I have never been so sober in my life! . . . Yes, it's a party, but the only reason I'm at it is because I feel sorry for him! . . . I'm not even drinking! . . . I feel sorry for him because he goes on licking the boot that has been kicking him in the crutch for thirty-eight years! . . . I am not being vulgar! I'm just trying to make you understand! . . . It has everything to do with me! I have joined this organization, for your sake, Jenny! And this is the kind of thing it does! . . . I know I haven't been here for thirty-eight years! But this man! You should see him! . . . He's completely knackered! . . . What? . . . All right! Right! Good-bye! (*He angrily slams the phone down*)

David Pulman comes in from the lift R

Pulman Hullo, there. How's it going?

Richard Very well, I think.

Pulman Thank you so much for doing what you did today.

Richard What did I do?

Pulman I always think it's so sad, on one's last day, to have no-one to talk to, all day long. Don't you?

Richard Oh, I see. Yes.

Pulman One tries to be kind. Good public relations.

The telephone rings on Veronica's desk

Where's Veronica? In the throng?

Richard I'll take it.

Pulman Thank you, Richard. Again.

Richard (*on the phone*) Hullo, Mr Pulman's office. . . .

Veronica enters her office

Yes. . . .

Veronica (*in the doorway*) Don't bother. I'll take it.

Richard Yes. . . . Is that the whole of the message? . . . Yes, I will. Good-bye. (*He hangs up*)

Pulman Tidings?

Richard The Chairman's secretary. The Chairman can't come. Will we tell Ken Grist?

Pulman Well, Richard, since you've taken the message, you'd better deliver it.

Richard Yes.

Pulman Privately or publicly, do you think? (*He goes into his own office*) Hullo, Ken.

Grist (*seeing Pulman coming in*) Aha! The Great White Chief! Let me get you a drink!

Pulman So sorry I'm late. Unforgivable.

Grist Here's your scotch, and I've made it a big one!

Pulman Thank you, and cheers.

Grist (*taking Pulman aside*) David, can I just have a quiet word with you? Have you seen the Chairman?

Pulman Not since this morning. Why?

Grist D'you think he's coming?

Pulman He said he was coming, this morning.

Grist D'you think I ought to ring his office, to make sure?
Pulman Oh, no. He won't have forgotten.
Grist It's just that—you know—he said he was coming, but . . .
Pulman Ken, you know the Chairman better than I do. A lot better.
Grist Yes . . .
Pulman He's a man of his word. If he says a thing, he does it.
Grist Yes . . .

In her office Veronica, amused, has been looking at Richard, who stands appalled

Veronica Good Public Relations? Speech?

Richard looks at her and makes his decision. He walks quickly into the party. Veronica follows

Richard (*loudly*) May I have your attention please! Please!
Grist Ay-ay! Young Dick! Pray silence for the newest member of Greatrick!

They listen to Richard

Richard It's just that, since I am the newest member, I take messages. A message from the Chairman's office, just now, to Ken Grist.

Grist's face is full of anxiety

And I thought you'd all like to hear it. The message is—and I repeat it word for word . . .
Grist Well done, that man!
Richard "Please tell my old friend Ken Grist I wanted very much to be there! But I have been called away, at a moment's notice, to a meeting which will have very important consequences for the future of Greatrick! And that is the one and only thing that could possibly have stopped me coming! . . . Tell Ken from me, I shall never forget how much he did to help build up this company! And tell him I wish him all the best with whatever company is lucky enough to employ him in the future!" End of message!

Everyone applauds. Grist is weeping tears of sentimental joy. Richard is exhausted by the effort of improvisation

Pulman (*patting Grist on the back*) Well done, Ken.
Grist (*still weeping*) I'll never forget those words. As long as I live.
Pulman You should wear them like a badge of honour.
Veronica (*to Richard*) David will now come across and say, "Very good, Richard. Congratulations."
Grist As long as I live . . .

Pulman comes across to Richard

Pulman Very good, Richard. Many congratulations. (*And he strolls away*)
Veronica (*to Richard*) The great thing about the good old days: the Chairman cut their balls off—personally.
Richard (*a bit dazed*) What?

Veronica Now he hasn't got time. He delegates.

The Lights fade to a Black-out

SCENE 3

*Rodney Spurling comes along the corridor to Veronica's office and goes in.
Veronica is there, as bright as the morning. Pulman is sitting at his desk*

Spurling 'Morning, Veronica.
Veronica Good morning, Rodney. Do you want him?
Spurling If I could just have a minute with him, before the meeting . . .
Veronica Walk right in.
Spurling Thank you.

Spurling goes into Pulman's office. Pulman looks up from his desk

'Morning, David.
Pulman The *Guardian* thing?
Spurling Seven o'clock this morning.
Pulman Me too.
Spurling And again, the moment I walk into the office.
Pulman A pity he ever learnt to read. (*Calling*) Veronica, can we have some
coffee? (*To Spurling*) You want help.
Spurling I doubt if you can do anything.
Pulman Oh yes. I can do one of two things, in the vain hope of helping.

Veronica brings in the coffee-tray and pours two cups

Spurling Like what?
Pulman They are mutually exclusive. You must choose which.
Spurling Must?
Pulman I beg your pardon, I phrased that badly. Thank you, Veronica. I
mean, if you want me to do either of these things, please say so.
Spurling Try me.

Veronica returns to her desk

Pulman I can say to the Chairman, "You are driving your splendid and
valuable Press Officer quietly round the twist: Rodney Spurling, God
bless his soul, is on the verge of a nervous breakdown, he can't pick
up a telephone without trembling all over, and this is due to your
abominable habit—sir—of ringing him up at all hours of the day and
night but mostly at crack of dawn, simply because the *Guardian* or
whatever has made some idiotic misprint like Groatrick for Greatrick.
So would you for Christ's sake please stop doing it—sir."
Spurling Doesn't sound like you.
Pulman I give you the sense of what I would say. Not the words I would
use to say it.
Spurling Have you ever changed the Chairman's habits yet?
Pulman I'm willing to try.

Spurling Does the Chairman like employees on the verge of nervous break-downs?

Pulman Since he drives them there, I suppose he likes it. I don't suppose he likes being told it.

Spurling No.

Pulman You think no, to that one.

Spurling What's the other one?

Pulman Well . . .

Spurling Since you wanted me to say no to that one.

Pulman Entirely your choice.

Spurling Is it?

Pulman Do I make myself so clear?

Spurling You always make yourself clear.

Pulman Good. Or I can say to the Chairman, "Your splendid and valuable Press Officer is doing splendid-and-valuable work. You should pay him more money."

Spurling That sounds more like you.

Pulman Yes, it does, doesn't it? And it's the only practical way in which I can express my sympathy.

Spurling thinks this over

Spurling Can we leave it for a bit?

Pulman As you wish, Rodney. It's your problem more than mine.

Spurling Things may change.

Pulman The Chairman won't change. Will you?

Spurling I always come in here determined to get you to agree something. And go out having agreed something else.

Pulman I don't lift a finger. You do it yourself.

Spurling Do I?

Pulman One more chance. What did you come in here determined to . . .?

Spurling Can you stop the Chairman ringing me up at seven in the morning?

Pulman Shall we start again? I can do one of two things.

Spurling You can do one thing. More money.

Pulman I am ninety per cent certain I can get you more money.

Spurling Leave it till next week or so.

Pulman Your decision, Rodney.

Spurling Yes. (*He turns to go*)

Pulman Oh, would you ask Veronica to come in?

Spurling Sure.

Pulman Thank you, Rodney.

Spurling goes out to Veronica's office and exits up R

Spurling (*as he passes through Veronica's office*) Veronica.

Veronica goes into Pulman's office

Pulman Veronica, if you ever see me getting like Rodney, will you remind me it's time to move to another job?

Veronica I don't see you getting like Rodney.

Pulman I am lucky to have no wife.

Veronica She's a good wife.

Pulman No. She loves him too much. She suffers because he suffers. And he suffers, watching her suffering.

Veronica Yes. But they're both masochists.

Pulman In that thing I'm supposed to be writing for that stupid magazine, about the qualifications needed for a successful executive . . . What was my list?

Veronica (*remembering*) One, intelligence. Two, flexibility. Three, self-control . . .

Pulman Stop. Insert a new Number Two. High frustration tolerance.

Veronica And downgrade everything else?

Pulman Downgrade everything else.

Eve, Frame, Spurling and Richard come into Veronica's office

Veronica Ah, they're coming. Are you ready for them?

Pulman Ready, aye ready.

Veronica goes to the door

Veronica Do go in.

They come into Pulman's office, greeted by Pulman, and seat themselves round the desk

Pulman 'Morning, Eve, you're looking marvellous. 'Morning, Peter . . .

Frame 'Morning, David.

Pulman 'Morning, Richard—how's it going?

Richard Fine, thanks.

Pulman Fine. 'Morning, Rodney—no, I've seen you already, haven't I? (*To Veronica*) Are we all here? It seems rather few.

Veronica Johnny Watt is in Hartlepool—and Malcolm is buried in his project.

Pulman Heaven forbid we should disinter him. Veronica, no calls. Except the irresistibly important ones.

Veronica Right.

Eve And Ken Grist is no longer with us.

Pulman And Ken is no longer with us.

Eve Heaven be praised?

Pulman Oh, I don't think heaven comes into it. Shall we start from that point? Peter, I think you wanted to . . .?

Frame (*about to make an important announcement*) Yes, I do. (*He rises*)

Pulman As our new Assistant Director . . .

Frame May I say, David—although I'm officially taking over the title of A.D.P.R., and the office and so on, I know you absolutely agree with me, I hope all of you do, titles are meaningless, especially in Public Relations, what matters is clarity of conception, the conception of the task. What I should like to try is something very different—from—er . . .

Eve The dear departed.

Frame From Ken's way of doing things. What I should like, David has promised to give it a go, I hope you all will, I should like you all to look on me, not as Assistant Director or anything like that, but look on me as—as a think-tank . . .

Eve I never look on you as anything else.

Frame As for conception—well, since this Department is so close to the centre of power—inevitably, it's concerned with the public expression of company policy at the highest level, we ourselves play a large part in shaping if not the policy then certainly the expression of it, and the expression *is* the policy, the medium is the message and all that—since this Department is necessarily therefore in daily close, you might say intimate, contact with the—the . . .

Eve Almighty?

Frame Don't joke, Eve. With the Chairman——

Eve Wasn't joking.

Frame —and since the Department is already deeply enmeshed in the function of industrial relations, interpreting the company to its employees through the news bulletins and the house magazine—and in the whole function of selling, who else but us presents an image of the company to the public at large, and these days one is selling not so much a product as an image, an ideal, so long as the product can be made to seem to resemble the ideal in the public's mind—and of course selling determines production, you know as well as I do, one doesn't sell what one makes, one makes what one sells . . . So this Department should move from being a link to being a control—Personnel and Works Relations, Advertising, Sales and Marketing, yes, Production too, all these things are essentially and properly parts of a Public Relations operation.

Frame collapses in his chair. A silence

Pulman Thank you, Peter. And well done.

Frame (*exhausted*) Thank you.

Pulman Comments please? Eve?

Eve I think junior member first, don't you?

Pulman Richard, you?

Richard I thought it was marvellously thought-provoking.

Eve Not to mention life-enhancing?

Richard But I'm very new boy here. I should like time to ponder.

Pulman Of course. The point is to ponder. Eve, you now?

Eve I should like to ponder too. Thank you, Richard. I like that word.

Pulman Rodney?

Spurling Well, I do have one question.

Pulman Out with it.

Spurling I understand about Peter being a think-tank—I mean, he's a natural think-tank . . .

Frame Thank you.

Spurling Can I ask you something?

Frame Anything.

Spurling Ken Grist used to sign our expense-sheets. Will it be you from now on?

Frame Yes.

Spurling (*making a note on a piece of paper*) Right. That's all.

Eve Can I ask something, too? Now that I've pondered a bit?

Pulman Please do.

Eve In order to help me with further pondering?

Pulman Eve, dear, stop building up to your punch-line.

Eve Not a punch-line at all. It's just—was Ken Grist fired . . .?

Pulman Technically, Ken was fired. It helped him with his severance pay.

Eve Ah. I didn't think of that.

Pulman I did.

Eve And what a clever answer.

Pulman Yes. And truthful.

Eve What a pleasure it must be to combine the two.

Pulman Yes, it is.

Eve Was Ken technically or otherwise fired in order to clear the way for a massive reorganization of the Department . . .

Frame Reorientation rather than reorganization.

Pulman Eve, I shall be delighted to explain to you, in detail, but later on in the day, perhaps? I have a minor question put to me by the Chairman, and like all minor questions put by the Chairman, it takes precedence over all questions put by anyone else. Now that the company has expanded, diversified, etcetera, etcetera . . . "Greatrick Limited" hardly seems important enough.

Spurling It's his name, doesn't he like it?

Pulman He does not propose to lose his name from the title.

Spurling Greatrick Unlimited?

Pulman We are now the Greatrick Organization.

Spurling Ah.

Pulman Like it?

Eve Funny, without being the least bit vulgar.

Pulman The burning question is, an Ess in Organization, or a Zed?

Eve Zed is American. I mean Zee is American.

Pulman It is also *Oxford English Dictionary*. Richard, would you do a short paper? Usage, here and elsewhere? Advantages, disadvantages?

Richard Right.

Pulman By—let's be generous—first thing tomorrow morning?

Richard Right.

Spurling (*to Richard*) Whatever you come up with will be wrong.

Pulman Now. I saved the best till last. The most important item for many a long week. You all, I think, know, or know of, Doctor Ducker.

Spurling Know of.

Richard Know of.

Eve Know only too much of.

Spurling His fame has spread from the provinces.

Eve Doctor Ducker has cut a swathe through our far-flung dominions, the like of which has not been seen since Attila the Hun.

Pulman What do you know about him?

Eve Not so much about him as about the effect of him. Strong men reel and faint when he walks into the room.

Pulman Is he so frightening?

Spurling The fear is in themselves.

Pulman Ah.

Spurling Every executive in this organization knows, deep down in his soul, not merely that he is incompetent at his job, but also that his job is, in itself, unnecessary. And that some day someone is going to see this.

Pulman Including you, Rodney?

Spurling I say to myself first thing every morning, "Today is the day they find me out".

Pulman Doctor Ducker will be with us on Monday, for a week.

Eve To investigate us?

Pulman To study our operation, and report on it.

Eve Your distinctions get so subtle sometimes. All Headquarters?

Pulman Starting with us.

Eve Wow!

Pulman The Chairman hired Doctor Ducker because of the wonders he did for the United Tobacco Company. Following his report, United Tobacco streamlined its entire organization, set up a Team Improvement programme, a Goal Orientation programme and a Job Satisfaction programme . . .

Spurling Fired two whole Departments . . .

Frame No. Not true.

Spurling I know some of the people.

Frame Not true at all, Rodney. It did happen that some employees were found to be redundant.

Spurling Yes.

Frame But Ducker's report—I saw a copy of it—did not recommend the elimination of two Departments. What it did recommend was the amalgamation of three Departments into one.

Spurling Subtle distinction?

Frame Which is why I myself look on this visit by Ducker—who is after all the leading man in his field—as being a great challenge, and a great opportunity, for this Department.

Pulman Peter will be in charge of the visit. If anyone is ever in charge of Doctor Ducker.

Frame If I can just say this—to help you with your approach—Ducker is essentially an expert diagnostician. He diagnoses—defines—functional disorders. He puts his finger on the spot.

Eve Ouch.

Frame Since I believe that this Department functions marvellously well— and is in fact the central powerhouse of the whole Organization . . .

Eve You want us to be nice to him.

Frame I simply want you to be your essential selves.

Eve Uh-huh.

Pulman You, Rodney, with your transparent integrity—Richard, your boyish charm—Eve, your feminine . . .

Eve Wiles?

Pulman Intuition.

Frame Disparate elements making a harmonious whole. And *functioning* . . .

Pulman I won't ask for comments—any questions, not too jokey?

Spurling Just one.

Pulman Yes, Rodney?

Spurling Where will you be while this is going on?

Pulman Regrettably, I have to fly to New York for a week . . . (*He smiles benevolently at their expressions of disbelief*) What is the head of a well-functioning Department, if he cannot delegate? I leave you in the safe, strong hands of Peter Frame. Thank you, all. (*He rises, as a signal that the meeting is over*) Eve, would you like to stay behind for a moment?

They all replace their chairs

Eve Sure.

All exit except Eve and Pulman, and Veronica, who goes to work in her office

Pulman And a very good day to the rest of you . . . (*When they have gone*) I promised you an explanation about Ken Grist.

Eve You've thought of one?

Pulman It has to be good, for you.

Eve I'd rather have the truth.

Pulman Any truth you want.

Eve Not any truth. The.

Pulman All right, if you insist. The.

Eve Yes.

Pulman Truth.

Eve Yes.

Pulman History. The Chairman wanted a Public Relations Department, to do something for his image. I'm an expert on images. So he took me on, from outside. But he doesn't trust people from outside. They haven't been trained.

Eve They haven't been knackered.

Pulman Two birds with one stone. Ken was useless in Sales Department. But a faithful watchdog. To make sure I didn't pee without asking the Chairman's permission.

Eve May not be true but it's good stuff so far.

Pulman Comes the time when I am trained. Knackered. Good Greatrick Head of Department. The Chairman rings me up on a Sunday—you know that terrible habit he has. "Is it possible to speak to you? David, I've been thinking, you ought to promote Peter Frame. Clever chap. Good ideas." "Certainly, sir. What shall I do with Ken?" "Who?" "Ken Grist, sir." "Oh, him. He's no use to you, is he?" "No, sir." "Fire him."

Eve You should go on the halls. Great mimic.

Pulman Thank you.

Eve Boy, you really are knackered. As knackered as Ken Grist.

Pulman I think sometimes—often—it's my job to be knackered.

Eve You know, what I really admire about you . . . Other people, they say what's in the front of their minds, I can guess what's in the back of their minds. You . . . Sometimes I think you have a back behind the back. And sometimes I think you've done the neatest switch of the week. You put the back at the front and the front at the back. You say what you really mean, to make us disbelieve it. Or what you obviously don't mean, because you want us to guess your secret.

Pulman Oh, what a clever chap I am.

Eve Oh, what a clever chap you are.

Pulman acknowledges this with a bow, and exits

Eve makes a half-mocking bow in return, and goes out to Veronica's office

Veronica, when did he fix up the New York trip?

Veronica Weeks ago. Why?

Eve And when did he fix up the Ducker visit?

Veronica Oh, that wasn't arranged by him.

Eve No?

Veronica It's just that, when he was given the dates for the Ducker visit, he forgot to remember the New York trip.

Eve And you forgot to remind him.

Veronica Yes, I know I should have. It was my fault. I forgot.

Eve When's he back?

Veronica It's a bit vague.

Eve Try this one on for size? Doctor Ducker is a humourless fanatic. It might be best to face him with another, equally, or even more so . . .

Veronica You mean Peter?

Eve I am trying to see into David's mind, through a glass, darkly . . . If that way works, all well and good. If it doesn't, that's Peter's fault. And there may still be time to rush back and pull the chestnuts out of the fire.

Veronica I don't think there's any thought of that.

Eve And we burn?

Eve goes out by the stairs L

The Lights fade to a Black-out

SCENE 4

Veronica is working in her office

Frame comes out of the lift R *with Doctor Ducker, who is quiet and professorial, with a disconcertingly steady gaze. Frame goes along the corridor to the private entrance to Pulman's office*

Frame And David did suggest you might like to use his office while he's away. It is of course terribly central, the hub of all our activity—myself near at hand, Rodney and Eve across the corridor, Veronica at your fingertips . . .

They enter Pulman's office

Of course it's entirely up to you. But I do feel that you should feel, what shall we say, in the thick of it.

Ducker David?

Frame David Pulman.

Ducker All Christian names? Throughout?

Frame A symbol of our system. We are very much a working democracy. David is of course first among equals, but the Department does essentially function as a group, a co-operative, decisions are made by consensus of opinion, with David Pulman or, in his absence, myself, acting as, how shall I put it, as moderator . . . Since you'll be with us all week, I do hope you'll come to our Friday morning conference, where we all gather together and kick things back and forth, with no respect for anything but the *goal* . . .

Ducker Secretaries' Christian names, too?

Frame Of course. Of course.

Ducker Both ways?

Frame Well, actually mine happens to be very new, she hasn't yet got used to . . . But . . . (*He goes quickly to Veronica's door*) Veronica?

Veronica (*coming in quickly*) Yes, Peter?

Frame There!

Ducker Yes.

Frame Veronica, may I introduce Doctor Ducker . . .

Veronica Hullo.

Ducker Hullo.

Frame (*to Ducker*) Veronica will look after you, typing and telephone calls and so on.

Veronica Anything you need.

Frame Just say the word.

Ducker Thank you, but I don't think I need anything.

Frame Well . . . Thank you, Veronica. Wonderful girl, Veronica. Totally dedicated.

Veronica gives them a smile and goes back to her desk

If I could start by explaining the fundamental creed of this Department—the basic theory that underlies all our practice . . .

Ducker I think practice first, don't you?

Frame As you wish . . .

Ducker I do tend to find that if one observes the practice, one can perfectly well deduce the underlying theory.

Frame Yes, I suppose . . .

Ducker I mean the real theory. Not the pretend one.

Frame Ah, yes . . .

Ducker Sometimes they're the same. Not often. Don't you find?

Frame Yes, I entirely agree.
Ducker Self-deception. The great sin of modern industry. Autocracies which believe themselves democracies. Hereditary dynasties which believe themselves elective. Superfluity which believes itself essential.
Frame Yes, well, I do think you'll discover, here, in this Department, that we do very much *function* . . .

But Ducker has turned away to consult a small notebook

Ducker Can I start by seeing your—(*he looks it up*)—your Mr Spurling?
Frame Of course. Of course. (*He quickly goes to Veronica's doorway*) Veronica, could you ask Rodney to come in here, please? To talk to Doctor Ducker? (*He returns to Ducker*)
Veronica Right. (*She dials an internal number*) Daphne? . . . Veronica. Would you ask Rodney to come to David's office? For Doctor Ducker? . . . Yes, I should think so. Would you get them to put calls through here?
Frame Rodney—Rodney Spurling, that is—handles our entire relationship with the daily and weekly press. With the help of, er, his secretary and, er, one other girl who does the library and press cuttings and so forth . . . Of course, if something big blows up, we all muck in and help out, bringing our united brains to bear—and of course there is constant consultation on policy—and on Friday mornings at the conference we all toss it back and forth, and make our contribution—a combination of talents all zeroing in on the same problem—we destroy it by the sheer energy of our brain-power . . .

Spurling hastens into Veronica's office down the stairs R

Spurling In there?
Veronica Yes.
Spurling What's he like?
Veronica Hm.
Spurling Oh well . . . (*He goes into Pulman's office*)
Frame Hullo, Rodney! Rodney Spurling, Doctor Ducker.
Spurling How d'you do?
Frame Doctor Ducker would like to talk to you . . .
Ducker No. Not talk.
Frame I have already explained to Doctor Ducker . . .
Ducker No. Please. No explanations. Not yet.
Frame I'm sure there'll be lots of questions he'll want to ask . . .
Ducker I think answers first, questions afterwards, don't you? (*Politely but dismissively*) Thank you, Mr Frame.
Frame Well, I'll—see you later . . .
Ducker Perhaps.
Frame Well . . . (*Reluctantly, he goes into Veronica's office*)

The phone rings on Veronica's desk

Veronica (*on the phone*) David Pulman's office. . . . Yes, he is, I'll put you through . . . (*She buzzes Spurling*)

Spurling (*on the phone*) Hullo?
Veronica (*on the phone*) Ted Shelley of the *Pictorial*.

Frame, believing that all is well, goes up the stairs R *and off*

During the following, Ducker places a chair very exactly, sits down on it, and gazes intently and unwinkingly at Spurling

Spurling (*on the phone*) Right. . . . (*To the caller*) Hullo, Ted, what d'you want now? . . . Ted, I've told you already, the next list of Birthday Honours is a matter between the Palace and the person. . . . Look, if you want to speculate, I can't stop you. I just think you're taking a risk. . . . My Chairman has a taste for sueing. He can afford to lose. . . . Yes, sure. . . . See you. Love to Helen. 'Bye. (*He hangs up. To Ducker*) You all right there?
Ducker Please behave as if you were in your own office, and as if I did not exist.
Spurling But I am not in my own office. And you do exist.
Ducker As if.
Spurling But even if you hid in a cupboard—so long as I knew you were there . . .
Ducker I make allowances for acting.
Spurling How do you know?
Ducker What?
Spurling How do you know how much is acting, due to your being there, since you can never be there to see what it's like when you're not there?
Ducker Please. As if.

The phone rings on Veronica's desk. She answers it

Veronica (*on the phone*) David Pulman's office. . . . Yes, hold on, please . . . (*She buzzes Spurling*)
Spurling (*on the phone*) Hullo? (*To Ducker*) As if.
Veronica (*on the phone*) Rodney, it's Miss Honeywell.
Spurling (*on the phone*) All right. . . . (*To the caller*) Rodney Spurling here. . . . Yes. . . . Yes. . . . Yes. . . . Yes, I understand the message perfectly. The Chairman wants an analysis tabulated, classified, based on the national papers over the last month, of what type of human in-terest stories got the best coverage. Would it be pointless to ask what the point of it is? . . . No, I don't want to talk to the Chairman—and he wants it by tomorrow afternoon? . . . Right. (*He hangs up, and looks at Ducker*) Doing my best. As if.

Ducker still gazes at him. Spurling takes a piece of paper and starts writing

Richard enters Veronica's office from the stairs R

Richard Will you have dinner with me tonight?
Veronica Shush!
Richard Why?
Veronica (*indicating where he is*) Doctor Ducker.

Richard Doesn't he approve of my taking you to dinner?
Veronica I had dinner with you last night.
Richard I want it to become a habit.
Veronica One condition.
Richard Any.
Veronica You are not to attempt to get me into your bed.
Richard Not even attempt?
Veronica No.
Richard As a heartfelt compliment?
Veronica Heartfelt?
Richard Felt. Strongly felt.
Veronica Tell me in words.

Spurling crumples up his piece of paper and throws it in the waste basket.
He takes another piece and more seriously starts writing

Richard Do you go to bed with David Pulman?
Veronica No.
Richard Why not? Him, or you?
Veronica Both.
Richard Both?
Veronica Rule for senior executives. Don't. Friendly but not too familiar.
Show her some well-chosen weaknesses, but not the real ones.
Richard And you?
Veronica Rule for secretaries. Don't. Unless you've decided to marry
him.
Richard And you haven't.
Veronica David looked in the mirror and married himself. A great mar-
riage.
Richard Can't compete with that.
Veronica No.
Richard It's the damnedest thing. It's the first time I've worked in a big
organization like this. Small company before, not the same thing.
But in this Greatrick—you get this extraordinary feeling that it—the
properly organized organization—sets out to fulfil the whole of its
employees' emotional needs. Whatever excitements, whatever happines-
ses, whatever satisfactions, whatever disappointments, whatever heart-
breaks—God knows, whatever orgasms—come from the relationship,
not between the employee and another human being, but between the
employee and the organization. Mistress, lover, wife, sweetheart, father,
mother, whatever you want, you can't want anything else, it's all pro-
vided. Do you know, since I joined Greatrick, I have not been capable
of thinking, or talking—it appals me—of anything except the people
here, and what goes on in the office?
Veronica I've been here longer than you have.
Richard Yes.
Veronica The same. Only more so.
Richard Christ.

Spurling buzzes Veronica

Veronica (*on the phone*) Yes, Rodney?
Spurling (*on the phone*) Veronica, could you possibly take a memo?
Veronica (*on the phone*) Sure. (*She hangs up. To Richard*) Dinner tonight.
Richard Great.

Veronica, with pad and pencil, goes into Spurling's office

Richard exits up R

Veronica Yes, Rodney?
Spurling Sorry to bother, but I should have done it yesterday . . .
Veronica That's all right. (*She sits*)
Spurling Memo to the Chairman, copies Pulman and Frame. Subject toy
  sales in Africa, dash, your memo of whatever the date was, Daphne
  will tell you. You ask me why I have not put out a press release about
  our toy sales to Africa. Paragraph. In my view the figures are not eye-
  catching enough to rate more than a brief mention on the business
  pages. If you want more than this, as I assume you do, I suggest we wait
  for next quarter's results which may show that we have doubled our
  sales of Golliwogs to Wogs or vice versa.
Veronica Do you think that last bit . . .?

*Spurling is in a state of extreme nervous tension, but not completely mad
yet*

Spurling Have doubled our sales of woolly animals or whatever may be
  thought newsworthy by London editors. That's it. All right?
Veronica A bit sharper than your usual.
Spurling Would you soften it for me? To make it the normal weak-
  kneed, servile . . . (*He cannot go on*)

Veronica looks at him, and decides not to say anything in front of Ducker

Veronica I'll be in my office. (*She returns to her desk*)
Spurling Are you comfortable there?
Ducker Yes.
Spurling I'm afraid I may be boring you.
Ducker No.
Spurling I'm afraid I may be about to bore you. I have to draft a very
  long memo . . .
Ducker Please do. As if.
Spurling For an hour or more. In dead silence. Wouldn't you rather go
  somewhere else, and watch someone else?
Ducker No, I'm very happy here.
Spurling Happy?
Ducker Yes.

*Spurling starts his drafting, in longhand on a foolscap pad. At the same time
Veronica starts typing his memo. Ducker continues to watch Spurling. Time
passes. Spurling can feel Ducker's eyes on him. He looks up and meets his
eyes. Ducker's eyes do not falter. Spurling goes on with his writing, but
more nervously twitching. Finally he can't stand it any longer. He puts*

down his pen and rises rapidly but rather unsteadily. Meanwhile, Veronica finishes typing the memo, and arranges it for presentation to Spurling for his signature

Spurling Excuse me. Got to see Peter Frame.

Spurling goes out to Veronica's office, just as Veronica is going to come in with the memo

Veronica Oh, Rodney . . .

Frame enters up R

Spurling Back in a moment. Gone to see Peter Frame. (*He goes quickly up the stairs, seizes Frame and takes him along the corridor*)
Frame Rodney—how's it going?
Spurling He is driving me out of my mind.
Frame But why?
Spurling No good reason. The only good reason, I can't stand it. That's all.
Frame Rodney, honestly, I do feel at times like this, so important for the Department——
Spurling I simply cannot stand it a moment longer.
Frame —the question of individual response to a personality, individual antagonism, should be put on one side——
Spurling It's not antagonism.
Frame —dispassionately, ruthlessly——
Spurling I just can't bear being watched.
Frame It's one of his techniques.
Spurling As if he were a sniper.
Frame A what?
Spurling Any moment, bing. Middle of my forehead.
Frame Rodney, we've all got to stay very calm.
Spurling That's what I'm saying. I can't.
Frame Try, Rodney. Please try.
Spurling If he goes on like this for the rest of the day, I shall scream and bite him in the leg.

Spurling turns and walks back into Veronica's office. Frame follows anxiously, at a distance

Veronica Oh, your memo. Would you like to sign it?
Frame Sign your memo, Rodney.
Spurling (*signing*) Thank you, Veronica. (*He returns to Pulman's office*)

Frame waits in Veronica's office

(*Suddenly stopping, and speaking to space again*) The old gag. First man to second man: "The reason you have an inferiority complex is because you are inferior." (*He sits and writes*)

No response from Ducker, who still watches. Spurling goes on with his writing for a moment, then lays down his pen. He buzzes Veronica

Veronica (*on the phone*) Yes, Rodney?
Spurling (*on the phone*) Veronica, no calls, please.
Veronica (*on the phone*) Right.

She and Spurling hang up

Frame What did he say?
Veronica "No calls please."
Frame What's happening? (*He waits, anxiously*)

At last Spurling looks at Ducker

Spurling I think you have by now seen the kind of thing I do all day long.
Ducker Yes.
Spurling I doubt if there's any great point in your going on observing me.
Ducker The point was, to bring us to this point.
Spurling Now that we've reached it—are there any questions you want to ask me?
Ducker I think the questions have answered themselves already, don't you?
Spurling Yes.
Ducker Unless you feel there's anything you want to say.
Spurling No.
Ducker Anything I might not have thought to ask questions about. If I had asked questions.
Spurling What might you not have asked questions about?
Ducker About what I don't know.
Spurling Forgive me. Most people do ask questions about what they don't know.
Ducker Yes, I think it's purposeless, don't you? If one really doesn't know the answer, one can't possibly frame an intelligent question. Nor test the validity of the answer.
Spurling You want to know the answer's right, before you ask the question?
Ducker It does make the answer so much more informative.
Spurling Yes.
Ducker Yes.
Spurling Well . . .
Ducker Well—if I've seen everything . . .
Spurling I imagine the usual effect of your technique is that the victims——
Ducker If you like.
Spurling —feel that they've represented themselves inadequately——
Ducker Do you? Imagine?
Spurling —and launch into a speech of self-justification.
Ducker Yes, usually.
Spurling Which is of course a dead give-away. Much more than anything else.
Ducker It tends to be.

Spurling I was wrong about you as a sniper. You don't shoot people, you wait for them to hang themselves.

Ducker Sometimes.

Spurling For purposes of clarification—do they all start like that?

Ducker Something like that.

Spurling And go on to explain how important and essential their job really is, whatever it may seem to be, to the eye of their observer.

Ducker Yes.

Spurling Leave aside for the moment the question of how important or essential. I and my staff spend our time doing three things. *First.* We answer queries from the press. The firm is a big one, my Chairman is a well-known public figure, we get a lot of queries. If the answer is a creditable one, I give it. If the answer is discreditable but there's no way of concealing it, then I try to put it in as good a light as I can. Sometimes I have the easy way out: I can simply reply I don't know. *Second.* I feed information to the press, of the kind that redounds to the glory of Greatrick. Instance the last few weeks. The manager of our toy factory at Shaddington doesn't expect a title like the Chairman, but he's working his arse off for an O.B.E. Local do-gooder. He's conned his workmen into doing half-an-hour's unpaid overtime, making toys for the local hospital. And he wants to have it known. *Third.* I explain to the Chairman, why that story didn't make a centre-page spread in the *Mirror*; or why an uncomplimentary remark about Greatrick did appear at the bottom of page fifteen in the *West Wittering Weekly*. This takes up most of my time. It's no good my saying I'm not the editor. I have to analyse, in depth, my own failure to get a thing printed or to stop a thing being printed. What purpose this serves, what good it does in the world, what good it does for Greatrick— is completely beyond me. Someone once said that all Press Officers— all P.R. Departments, come to that—should be abolished and replaced by one intelligent girl with a telephone, referring inquirers to the person responsible—who knows the answer and can give it, or not give it, as the case may be. In my opinion, my job is utterly unimportant and totally inessential. Does that answer the question you did not ask?

Ducker Yes. Very thoroughly.

Spurling Good. May I go now?

Ducker Yes. Thank you very much.

Spurling Thank *you*.

Spurling goes out to Veronica's office. Frame has been waiting there in a fury of anxiety. He rushes at Spurling

Frame Rodney. How did it go? Was it all right?

Spurling I told him I was unimportant and inessential.

Frame What . . . !

Spurling I said the whole Department was unnecessary.

Spurling goes on out of the room and away up R

Frame stares after him

Frame He's mad. He'll ruin us.

The phone on Veronica's desk rings

Veronica (*on the phone*) Hullo. . . . Oh, hullo.
Frame Veronica . . .
Veronica (*on the phone*) Hold on a moment, would you? (*To Frame*) Yes,
Peter?

Ducker exits through the private door and up the stairs L

Frame Get everyone together as soon as you can. We must have an emergency meeting. And get me David in New York. I must tell him—
Rodney's gone out of his mind.

Frame rushes up the stairs and exits R

Veronica is alone

Veronica (*on the phone*) Sorry, David, that was Peter. He wants me to get
you. . . . Yes, I think that would be very good timing.

The Lights fade to a Black-out

SCENE 5

*Frame is in Pulman's office, anxiously pacing. He has a script in his hand.
Eve, Richard and Veronica enter: Eve and Richard from up* R, *Veronica
into her office from her own door*

Veronica 'Morning, Eve.
Eve 'Morning, Veronica.
Veronica 'Morning, Richard.
Richard 'Morning, Veronica.

They file silently into Pulman's office

Frame I asked you all to come in, I do apologise if I've taken you away
from anything else, and Veronica too, because of course Veronica is
absolutely in David's confidence in this matter, I've just been talking
to David in New York, I've explained the whole thing, he does feel
that he's powerless to influence events at such a geographical distance,
and of course he's terribly tied up in meetings over there, but he'll be
in touch whenever he can, with me or through Veronica, and of course
he'll drop everything and rush back here if the crisis should develop
into a—and believe me the only word I can find for it is crisis, but if
it should escalate into an emergency . . . The simple fact is that Rodney,
this morning, with Doctor Ducker, went out of his mind.
Eve You mean, Doctor Ducker went out of his mind, too? .
Frame No. Not at all. Why?
Eve You said, "Rodney, with Doctor Ducker . . ."

Frame While he was with Doctor Ducker.

Eve Ah.

Frame Rodney went berserk. He denounced—denounced is the only word I can find—denounced his own work, and the entire work of the entire Department, as being totally unnecessary and totally dispensable. To Ducker.

Eve Well, you did ask him to be his essential self.

Frame Of course, we all know that Rodney is sensitive—highly strung— a man who lives on his nerves—very easily thrown off balance by what rightly or wrongly he feels to be a hostile or critical approach. Of course, I shall do my utmost to explain all this to Ducker. But however I put it, however far I succeed—the damage is done.

Richard "Oh God, put back thy universe and give me yesterday."

Frame Exactly. The Department—the continued existence of the Department—is in danger. Is at stake.

Richard Short of God putting his universe back, which seems on the whole unlikely . . .?

Frame I don't know how well up you are in Ducker's theories, as expounded in his book.

Eve Tried to read it, couldn't. I have a low threshold of boredom.

Richard I got through it, over the weekend.

Frame Then Richard at least will know, the basic concept, the nub of the whole thing, is decision-making by consensus. Co-operation. Functioning as a team, as a group. Rootedness in a stable group, and identification with that group. But the importance of Ducker's work is that he adds a rider, without departing from the principle of unity, group action, total harmony within the group, these are vital to the execution of ideas, to planning, to administration. But for the creation of ideas, for the group to act as a creative vehicle, it cannot operate by absolute consensus, it needs to contain, as a necessary part of its equipment, one active dissentient.

They get it, and they enjoy it

Eve Ah-hah.

Frame One person who disagrees, who questions, who challenges the very basis of the group's collective thinking.

Richard Rodney.

Frame Yes. Exactly. Thank you, Richard.

An appreciative silence

Veronica Rodney is the grain of sand without which there would be no pearl.

Eve Rodney is the discord without which there would be no resolution into harmony. Your turn, Richard.

Richard Rodney is the quarrel without which love would be boredom.

Eve Peter, you are a genius. No-one but you could have thought of it.

Frame If we all proceed on that principle, and believe me, we must, or we're done for—eliminated—amalgamated . . .

Eve I shall go and prepare my mind for that principle. It takes a bit of getting used to.
Frame Yes, well, that's all I have to say.
Eve You've said enough, Peter. This is your finest hour.

Eve goes out through Veronica's office and up L

Frame Richard, I think Ducker wants to see you next, I thought it might impress him if we showed him an example of how we work together, on that film script as a good example . . .
Richard Fine.
Frame If he saw us tossing it back and forth, stimulating each other, striking sparks off each other's ideas—but thinking in unison . . .
Richard Yes, sure. I'll go and get my copy of the script.

Richard goes out through Veronica's office and up R

Frame Splendid fellow, Richard.
Veronica Yes.
Frame I think he'll wipe out any unfortunate impression that Rodney may have made . . .

Ducker comes in up L *and through the private door*

Frame sees him

Thank you very much, Veronica, as quickly as possible.
Veronica Thank you, Peter. (*She goes to her office*)
Frame (*to Ducker*) I've asked Richard Pershore to come and meet you, since you do want to observe us at our normal work, as if you weren't here, and Richard is in fact due for a session with me.
Ducker Good.
Frame Richard Pershore is our newest recruit, but already marvellously loyal, and splendidly compatible, a great feeling of belonging here, a well-rounded peg in a well-rounded hole.
Ducker Oh yes? (*But he is showing no interest*)
Frame I should explain that we are in the process, in the early stages of making a film about the Organization, a documentary, a factual film, showing the whole scope, a special project, Richard's in charge of it, though of course he does confer constantly with myself, with David Pulman when he's here, in order to get the best possible . . . At the moment we're battling our way through a draft script, to make sure it's as honest, as vital, in cinematic terms, it expresses, it reflects, we are, after all, trying to hold a mirror up to nature, a moving mirror showing moving images . . .

Richard comes quickly into Veronica's office, a script in his hand. He is full of boyish charm

Richard Hullo, Veronica! (*He goes straight on into Pulman's office*) Hullo,

Peter! Here I am! Ready for work! (*Then he pretends to see Ducker*) Oh,
I beg your pardon . . .

Frame Richard, I don't think you've met Doctor Ducker, have you?

Richard How d'you do, sir?

Ducker How d'you do?

Frame Doctor Ducker will be here—as if he weren't here—while we have
our meeting . . .

Richard I say, what a good idea! Like a fly on the wall!

Frame We got to page ten yesterday, the beginning of the pensions
sequence . . .

Richard (*busily looking*) Page ten . . . Ah yes . . .

Frame I do think, in this sequence, I mentioned it yesterday, I don't know
if you thought about it overnight——

Richard I let it down into my subconscious. I'm afraid it hasn't come up
again yet.

Frame —it would feel so much more valid if the information were given
by the men themselves. The head of our Pensions Section, to most of
our employees, is a remote, impersonal figure. How can they feel,
how can they establish, with him, a meaningful connection? If he
appears on the screen and says, "This is what you get when you retire"—
the information is there, it's lucid, it's credible, but it doesn't carry a
punch, because it's not personalized. Whereas. You show a worker on
the screen, standing by his—lathe or whatever it is—and he looks up
from his—lathe or whatever—and says, in that hard, gritty, characterful
voice, I won't imitate the accent, "This is what *I* get when *I* retire".
You do so see that I is so much better than you.

Richard And in his home, perhaps? Cut from the lathe to the Council
flat?

Frame Not Council flat, they're so . . .

Richard Semi-detached.

Frame Better.

Richard With his wife and children. She takes up the tale.

Frame Exactly. She says, "And what is more, if my Bert, or whatever
his name is, dies while he is working for the Greatrick Organization",
and she explains how much he'll get.

Richard The only problem is accent.

Frame Yes, we shall have to be careful.

Richard If it's a Hartlepool worker they won't understand him in Pontypridd.

Frame There must be some of them who speak intelligible English.

Richard Might be better to hire professionals.

Frame No, no, they belong to amateur dramatic societies and things, we
can . . .

Richard Coach them. Rehearse them.

Frame Yes. But you do agree, the impact will be so much greater if we
re-angle the whole thing.

Richard The whole thing?

Frame I think so, don't you? We can kick this around at the Friday
morning conference. But why don't we make it, not statements by

management, not the impersonal voice of God on the soundtrack, but a series of interviews, intimate human interviews, with the actual men and women in the various factories and so on . . .

Richard And change the title.

Frame Yes. Something more . . .

Richard Personalized. "It's good to work at Greatrick." "It's great to work at Greatrick." Even before the main title comes on the screen. Fade in on a man working at his whatever. He looks up at the camera. Smiles. Winks. "Oh, ay," he says, intelligibly, but with enough local accent to give it authenticity and character, "It's great to work at Greatrick!" Bring in the title music.

Frame (*snapping his script shut*) Richard, I think we've discovered what the whole thing is about.

Richard Can we go on for a bit discussing what the whole thing is about?

Frame I think we should.

Richard If the film is to consist of the workers telling how great it is to work at Greatrick—good conditions, canteens, social clubs, sports clubs, pensions and so forth——

Frame Yes.

Richard —what is the point of making the film?

Frame What?

Richard Which I thought was for showing to the workers?

Frame goggles at him

I mean, what's the point of telling them something they already know? And they must already know, or we couldn't have made the film. The people on the screen are simply talking to themselves.

Frame The film would of course be seen by new entrants——

Richard —who presumably have joined Greatrick because of good conditions, canteens and so forth——

Frame (*a bit desperate*) —and would of course show what things are like at, say, Pontypridd, to the workers at, say, Hartlepool——

Richard —who presumably think they're exactly the same. As indeed they are. Peter, you do understand, I'm simply trying to challenge the basis of our thinking.

Frame (*wishing to God Ducker was not there*) Ah . . .

Richard Now, if the basis is wrong: if, as I tend to believe, the real purpose of making the film is for the Chairman and his Board of Directors to show it to themselves, in private, in an orgy of self-congratulation——

Frame Richard . . . !

Richard —then I do see the point of having workers saying how lucky they are.

Frame Richard, shall we start again by going back to the original brief, which was very carefully worked out . . . ?

Richard Honestly, Peter, whichever way you look at it, it does seem a terrible waste of money and time. Except, if there weren't any film, I wouldn't have anything to do. Shall we kick it around at the Friday morning conference?

Frame (*longing to get him out of the room*) Yes, that'd be the best thing . . .

Richard Can I say something to Doctor Ducker?

Ducker Please do.

Richard (*to Ducker*) Some people have been saying that the Department is unnecessary. I strongly deny this. The Department is necessary.

Frame Exactly. As a power-house.

Richard No. The Department is necessary because it employs me. Work exists to support the worker. That's all. No other consideration is involved.

With a brilliant smile for Ducker, Richard goes out to Veronica's office. Frame is left speechless. Richard gives Veronica another brilliant smile, and a word in passing

O frabjous day!

Richard goes out to the corridor, and meets Eve coming along towards Veronica's office from up L

Calloo callay! He chortled in his joy!

Eve And you've been with Doctor Ducker?

Richard I have made it abundantly clear to him that my work is totally unnecessary. I hope I have made it seem that Peter is largely unnecessary. I think I have implied that the Department is hardly necessary.

Eve gazes at him in wonderment and delight

Eve It's so beautiful. So simple. So simply beautiful. I can't possibly beat you. I'd better join you.

Richard exits up L

Eve moves on towards Veronica's office

Ducker (*to Frame*) Could I see the next person, please?

Frame Yes. Yes, of course. Just a moment. (*He rushes out to Veronica's office*) Could you get David in New York. Urgently. Richard's gone out of his mind.

Eve enters Veronica's office

Eve! Would you please, for Heaven's sake—for the Department's sake ... (*Then he sees that he left the door to Pulman's office open, and Ducker is standing in the doorway gazing at him*) Eve, I don't think you've met Doctor Ducker?

Eve Hullo, Doctor Ducker.

Ducker How d'you do?

Eve What's your Christian name?

Ducker Melvyn.

Eve I shall call you Doctor Ducker.

Ducker Won't you come in?

Frame (*ushering Eve into Pulman's office*) Yes, do come in. And tell Doctor Ducker about what you do here. I know you can be relied on——

Eve You think so?
Frame —to do that.

Eve sits, and looks at them

Eve (*to Ducker*) Are you going to watch me?
Ducker May I——
Eve I adore being watched.
Ducker —sit down?
Eve Oh, please. (*He sits and looks at her*) You're watching. That's nice. And now?
Ducker I think you're going to talk to me. Please talk.
Eve Doctor Ducker, you are a percipient fellow.
Ducker Yes.
Eve Some people end with self-justification, some start with it . . .
Ducker And some in the middle.
Eve I'm the kind who starts with it.
Ducker Yes.
Eve Of course you knew. Job definition?
Ducker Whatever you want to tell me.
Eve Mainly I am the editor—editress?—and chief scribe of the house bulletin and the house magazine. (*She calls*) Veronica!
Veronica (*from her office, coming to the doorway*) Yes, Eve?
Eve Have you got copies of the current bulletin and the magazine?
Veronica Yes, of course. (*She hurries to bring them from a filing cabinet*)
Eve Funny, most people make paper aeroplanes out of them.

Veronica brings her copies then sits down in Pulman's office

Thank you, Veronica. (*To Ducker*) Now the house bulletin, which I am holding between finger and thumb, and which just for fun is called *Greatrick News*, and you try and do better than that in two words, one of which has got to be Greatrick—am I going too fast for you? ——
Ducker No.
Eve —comes out once a year and on special occasions like Christmas, or the Chairman's birthday. The main purpose of the bulletin is to tell people what they already know. Example. I quote. (*She reads*) "Jean Bloodworthy, with Personnel for the last five years, has transferred to Sales Department." Now, she knows she's transferred. Her friends know she's transferred. And secondly, to tell people what they don't want to know. Useless information. Who except Jean Bloodworthy cares?
Ducker Mm.
Eve But the house magazine is an entirely different kettle of fish. (*She holds it up*) It smells different. Every month, handsomely printed, superbly illustrated, correctly spelt—little jokes at the bottom of the page when I've got nothing else to fill up with. And serving two quite distinct purposes, either of which would be sufficient justification in itself. It demonstrates, visibly, for all the world to see, that Greatrick is the kind of organization that has a house magazine. And it reminds the employees of Greatrick that they are employees of Greatrick. Who

knows, there might be somebody, somewhere, who habitually forgets
the name of his firm, and is found wandering in the streets, or at completely the wrong place.

*Frame cannot stand it a moment longer. He rushes at Veronica and drags
her out to her own office*

Frame Veronica. Did you get that call to New York?
Veronica It's no good ringing David now. He's in a meeting, an important
meeting. All tied up. I daren't disturb him.
Frame I'll take the responsibility. Get him now. He must come back. It's
escalated into collective madness. The whole Department is commit-
ting mass *hara-kiri*.

The Lights fade to a Black-out

SCENE 6

*Frame is pacing impatiently up and down in Veronica's office. Ducker is
sitting peacefully in Pulman's office. Veronica and Pulman come from the
lift L, he carrying travelling-bags, she carrying his briefcase and his light
raincoat. They come along the corridor and enter her office*

Frame David! Good trip?
Pulman Smooth as an American P.R. man. How are you?
Frame Oh God.
Pulman Veronica filled me in on the way from the airport. Shall we . . .

(He moves towards his own office)

Frame No, Ducker's in there.
Pulman Ah.
Frame For the Friday morning conference.
Pulman Of course.
Frame I've had time to think things over. While Ducker went away, to
digest his findings. But I've not the slightest doubt what his findings
will be. Unless you can do something. I've shot my bolt. I can't.
Pulman He'll recommend the abolition of the Department?
Frame He can hardly do otherwise. In some form or other—reduction to
a Section, amalgamation with Personnel . . .
Pulman Can I do something?
Frame I have the greatest respect for your powers.
Pulman Thank you, but hmm.
Frame *(picking up two envelopes from the desk)* You will find in the larger
of these envelopes my account of what each of them said to Ducker,
so far as I know. And my attempt at an analysis of why each of them
said what he did.
Pulman Ah. Good.
Frame Coming to the conclusion, the only one I could possibly come to—
that this man Ducker has, in some extraordinary way, managed to

brainwash each single one of them. He has somehow reduced them to zombies. Denying everything they normally believe when they're in their right minds.

Pulman D'you think I can un-brainwash them?

Frame I wonder if you and the others can, at the conference—can what—I don't know—pass the whole thing off as a practical joke.

Pulman Interesting thought.

Frame And make the whole conference a retraction . . . an expression of loyalty and solidarity . . . The smaller envelope is because I failed to do what you gave me to do. My resignation.

Frame puts the second envelope into Pulman's hands, and marches out and away like a soldier, to exit up R

Pulman I don't think the time has come to accept his resignation yet.

Veronica When will it be?

Pulman *I* should like to choose the moment and the reason. (*He opens the door to his own office and goes in*) Ah, Doctor Ducker, I presume. I'm David Pulman.

Veronica sits at her desk

Ducker How d'you do?

Pulman I take it you're here to observe our Friday morning conference.

Ducker Yes.

Pulman I do hope there's something for you to observe. If you would care to sit . . . (*He gestures at a chair*)

Ducker Anywhere?

Pulman Do, please. Sit anywhere. (*He indicates his own chair*) Except here.

Eve, Spurling and Richard come from up R into Veronica's office, and continue towards Pulman's office

Eve (*as she passes through, to Veronica*) We who are about to die salute you.

Veronica You seem remarkably cheerful.

Eve Pain-killing drugs. So we won't feel the knife. (*She leads them on into Pulman's office*) 'Morning, boss!

Pulman 'Morning, Eve, 'morning, Rodney, 'morning, Richard. Do all sit anywhere. (*He indicates his own chair*) Except here.

Frame comes quickly into Veronica's office, and into Pulman's office

Frame Good morning.

Pulman 'Morning, Peter. I think that's all. Are you ready to begin the rain-dance?

A short pause. They all sit

Eve I like it. Did you bring it back from New York?

Pulman Yes.

Ducker The what?

Pulman Rain-dance. American metaphor. The traditional rituals which we still perform. Not because they produce rain, but because it would be deeply embarrassing to admit that they do not.

Ducker Ah, I see.

Pulman Now, what shall we have as the first item on the agenda?

While Pulman is saying this, Veronica dials an outside number

Veronica (*on the phone*) Malcolm? David Pulman to speak to you, hold on . . . (*She puts the phone down and runs to the main office*)

Pulman Perhaps we should start with . . .

Veronica David, I'm terribly sorry, Malcolm on the phone, it's important, could you speak to him? (*She runs back to her own phone*)

Pulman Yes, of course. (*Generally*) Excuse me. (*He lifts his phone*)

Veronica (*on her phone*) Malcolm? I'm putting you through now.

Pulman (*on his phone*) Hullo, Malcolm! How are you? Haven't seen you for a long time! What have you been up to? . . . Hold on a moment, Malcolm. I've got some people here, I'd like to explain . . . (*He puts his hand over the mouthpiece, to Ducker*) Malcolm is writing the official history of the Greatrick Organization. He's been writing it for . . . (*On the phone*) Is it two and a half years now, Malcolm? . . . (*With his hand over the mouthpiece, to Ducker*) Three years . . . (*On the phone*) Why is that, Malcolm? . . . Yes. . . . Yes, I see. . . . Hold on again, Malcolm. . . . Would you mind repeating that to somebody here? I'd very much like him to hear it. (*He again puts his hand over the mouthpiece and speaks to Ducker, indicating the phone on the coffee-table*) Would you pick up the phone down there?

Ducker picks up the phone

Ducker (*on the phone*) Hullo?

Pulman (*on the phone*) Go ahead, Malcolm!

Ducker (*on the phone*) Yes. . . . Yes. . . . Yes. . . .

Pulman (*on the phone*) Tell me, Malcolm, would you describe your work as unnecessary? . . . Oh. You would prefer the word "futile". Thank you, Malcolm! (*He hangs up*)

Ducker (*replacing the phone*) Mr Pulman, he said "It will never be finished. When it is finished it will never be printed. When it is printed it will never be published." Can you explain? (*He sits*)

Pulman Malcolm writes a draft of a chapter, and gives it to me. I make comments, in anticipation of the Chairman's comments. Malcolm rewrites the draft, gives it to me, I give it to the Chairman. He gets it back, smothered in amendments—I can never anticipate one-tenth of the Chairman's comments. He rewrites it, gives it to me . . . Need I go on?

Ducker No.

Pulman Doctor Ducker, you have heard us claim—proclaim—that we and our work are unimportant, unnecessary, futile, we serve no purpose.

Ducker Yes, that's right.

Pulman I myself—not that I can write your report for you—would add a rider to that. We are futile and unnecessary, except in so far as we help to conceal the fact that the Chairman is futile and unnecessary. Our work is in response to his desires. If he ceased to exist, we too would cease to exist.

Ducker I take the point. It has a certain value.

Pulman Further. We serve no purpose, because the Organization serves no purpose.

Ducker Except that of making money.

Pulman Yes. Our purpose is to disguise that purpose. And I'm very glad you've seen such a unanimity of opinion on this subject—a solidarity in our attitude towards the Organization, which one might define as ... I offer a prize for the best definition ...

Spurling Discontented servitude.

Eve Rebellious serfdom.

Richard Hostile subservience.

Pulman (*to Ducker*) I think Richard by a short head, don't you?

Ducker Yes.

Pulman Next on the agenda, I thought we might discuss the other means by which Chairmen seek to conceal their inadequacies, such as by hiring consultant psychologists ...

Ducker Mr Pulman ...

Pulman A question?

Ducker A statement. You are very talented people.

Pulman Thank you. Would you say the meeting has come to an end?

Ducker Yes, I think so.

Pulman (*generally*) Thank you, one and all.

The meeting starts to break up, in good spirits. Frame goes to Pulman

Frame I sat horror-struck. By the abysmalness of my own failure.

Pulman Oh, can I give you back your smaller envelope? (*He offers it*) Or shall I just tear it up?

Frame What?

Pulman Peter, you are a vital part of our equipment. The one non-co-operative member. The necessary dissentient.

Ducker Clearest example I've ever seen.

Pulman The grain of sand without which there would be no pearl.

Frame stares at them, while Pulman tears up the resignation. The Lights fade to a Black-out, as—

the CURTAIN *falls*

ACT II

SCENE 1

The same. The reversed lettering GREATRICK across the back window has been changed to reversed ORGANIZATION

Veronica, Spurling, Eve and Richard are all sitting round in the main office. Pulman is also there, sitting in his own chair at his desk—facing directly upstage, with his back to all of them

Eve (*indicating the pensive Pulman*) What cat has dared to get his tongue?

Veronica He's being unusually pensive.

Eve Yes, why?

Veronica I've no idea.

Eve Veronica, when did you last have no idea?

Veronica I think he'll come out with something sooner or later.

Pulman (*turning to face them*) Doctor Ducker has written his report—has written his behavioural, psychologist-management-consultant-expert-diagnostician report on the Organization—this most brilliant report, putting his finger on the essential, the central, weakness . . .

Frame hurries in up R and through Veronica's office

Eve Ouch already.

Pulman Of course we all knew it, but this man, comes in, takes one look, and states it more clearly than we ever did.

Frame (*entering Pulman's office*) So sorry. Terribly sorry, David, couldn't get away from, you know how it is, inter-departmental thing, about nothing at all, but I was trying to, for the sake of . . .

Pulman Yes, Peter, do sit down.

Frame (*sitting, generally*) Terribly sorry. Has David . . . ?

Pulman I quote from Ducker's major overall comment on this Organization we work for . . .

Frame Ah!

Pulman What oft was thought, but ne'er so well expressed . . .

Frame (*to whoever's next*) Marvellous man. Great brain.

Pulman After a rather jargony paragraph about the inevitably outmoded management style in a paternalistic autocratic structure . . .

Eve What?

Pulman It goes on—I quote—"The prime fault of the Organization is twofold. One, too much criticism downwards, which inhibits initiative and stultifies performance. Two, lack of criticism upwards, which encourages the leader in the delusion that he is infallible."

Eve Ducker, come back to us. All is forgiven.

Pulman "The remedies are obvious. Less criticism downwards. More upwards."

Eve Ducker, I love you.

Pulman "I strongly recommend. One, total cessation of criticism downwards for an initial period of six months. Two, immediate holding of criticism-upwards sessions, at which the leader is forcibly made to see how his subordinates see him."

Richard Phew!

Frame Brilliant. Absolutely right.

Eve I do hope that Doctor Ducker got paid his fee by the Chairman before the Chairman read the report.

Pulman You think Ducker made his meaning clear.

Spurling Except he did not say "The Chairman".

Pulman Mm . . .

Eve The leader, *Il Duce*, *Der Führer*, Jairman for Chairman, German for Cherman. Who else?

Frame Of course. Perfectly clear.

Pulman Eve, I am about to tell you the sickest joke you ever heard.

Eve Try. You've got competition.

Pulman I received—all Heads of Department got the same thing, I checked with them all—my copy of the report from the Chairman. The bits I've read out to you are sidelined in red ink. And with that same damned red pen of his, which is dipped in my heart's gore, an instruction. "See that these recommendations are carried out immediately within your Department."

They are caught between wild amazement and wild amusement

Frame No. It's not possible.

Pulman Not possible, but true.

Eve Boy oh boy oh boy.

Pulman Exactly.

Frame Absolutely absurd, when the whole point of Ducker's report was, I mean, that lunatic Chairman of ours, how could he possibly not have seen, the whole thing aimed at him, quite specifically, the one man in the Organization who must be brought to his senses, plain as a pikestaff. The man's mad.

Spurling No. He can prove that Ducker's words don't apply to him.

Frame How?

Spurling Internal evidence. The Chairman does not have delusions that he's infallible. He is infallible.

Frame Ah.

Eve Poor Ducker.

Spurling The delusions person must be somebody else.

Eve And poor David.

Pulman I throw myself on your mercy, since I have nowhere else to throw myself.

Frame Absolutely monstrous thing to do.

Pulman Yes, Peter, but what else do you suggest?

Frame I didn't mean you.

Pulman I am—the first time for some years—totally powerless. I am forbidden to criticize you. You are commanded to criticize me. All I can say to you is, shoot me like a soldier, do not hang me like a dog. Immediate holding of sessions, at which I must be forcibly made to see. Veronica will organize a date and time convenient to you all—please, Veronica?

Veronica Right.

Pulman With which thought—ladies—gentlemen—I bid you farewell for the moment. (*His farewell gesture is almost an obeisance*)

They rise and go silently: Eve and Richard up L, *Frame and Spurling up* R

Veronica is left with Pulman

Pulman I thought I was rather good, did you like me?

Veronica I thought you were rather hammy towards the end.

Pulman I never could resist acting.

Veronica No. I'm not on your side in this.

Pulman Whose side are you on?

Veronica Mine.

Pulman (*after a long pause*) Veronica, you are already paid as much as any secretary in this Organization.

Veronica One exception.

Pulman Who has been with the Chairman for twenty years. Who knows where the bodies are buried. She carried the shovel.

Veronica Yes. You do see my problem.

Pulman (*sighing*) If only to prove my desire to keep you, will you arrange for me to have lunch with the head of Personnel department.

Veronica I have, one o'clock today, Savoy Grill.

Pulman Call no man happy till he's dead. (*He goes to the drinks cabinet and pours himself a sherry*)

Veronica David, I'm starting a new thing. New school.

Pulman Good luck.

Veronica The face-value theory.

Pulman Mm?

Veronica People say what they think. Mean what they say. Do what they do for the reasons they say they do.

Pulman Veronica—it'll never catch on.

Veronica Why not?

Pulman When all the world is lying, only an idiot tells the truth.

Veronica It can be the cleverest thing to do.

Pulman You aren't talking about people saying what they mean because it's clever.

Veronica I'm talking about not wasting time. If you say what you mean you simply say it, no planning involved, no time wasted at all. But most of the people here spend half their time working out what they're going to say, and the other half working out afterwards whether they said the right thing. And the other half—all right, they've got three halves to their time—endlessly discussing, when the boss said "Good morning", did he mean it? And when he smiled, was it real, or are you out on your ear tomorrow?

Pulman (*replacing his empty glass*) Nevertheless, as a non-believer in your theory . . . Veronica, if over the next few weeks I seem more than usually . . . I can't think of the word, what am I usually?

Veronica Devious?

Pulman If I seem more than usually devious, you will realize, it is now partly for your sake?

Veronica Are you going to cheat?

Pulman Veronica, you know I never cheat. Except when it's my duty to cheat.

The Lights fade to a Black-out

SCENE 2

Pulman is at work in his office. Eve and Richard come along the corridor towards Veronica's office, and stop at the coffee-machine

Eve Coffee. To warm us for our task.

Richard What task?

Eve Today's the day the teddy-bears have their picnic.

Richard Criticizing David.

Eve Yes.

Richard I'm not going to be much use to you, at the picnic.

Eve Career?

Richard No.

Eve Caution?

Richard No, I don't think it's that.

Eve I wouldn't dream of saying, cowardice?

Richard There's a very good explanation for what I am going to do. It's just that I haven't found it out yet.

Eve You are in what my mother used to call a funny mood. Funny without being the least bit amusing.

Richard I am fed up because I've been with this Organization long enough now to know that I've been with this Organization long enough now.

Eve Quite liked that. Another try?

Richard And I am fed up because it makes me feel fed up to feel fed up.

Eve Still not quite getting there.

Richard I am fed up because I don't even love myself any longer.

Eve That is the most terrible thing a man can say. Drink up your coffee. Have some more. Have anything.

Richard You're great, you get rid of your problems by saying them. You'll go in there and tell David Pulman what you think of him, and feel better for having done it. Good reason. That's fine. I can't do it.

Eve My problem is, actually, I simply can't keep my trap shut.

Richard Your problem is, you're a marvellous, warm, breathing, human, infinitely human woman.

Eve That's not a problem, that's just the cross I have to bear.

Richard Why aren't you married?

Eve Tried it once, didn't like it.

Richard To—I don't know. An Emperor. I see you as a kind of improved version of Catherine the Great.

Eve There was room for improvement.

Richard Eve the Great. Little mother of all the Russias.

Eve The rushers and the pushers and the halt and the lame. And here come two of them.

Frame and Spurling enter up R *and come down into Veronica's room*

Frame 'Morning, Eve. Are you ready for the . . .? Ridiculous idea, I suggest we get it over with as soon as possible, in any case I have a . . .

Eve I want it to last for hours.

Spurling How you feeling, Eve?

Eve Like a teddy-bear.

Spurling Teddy-bear?

Eve Going down in the woods tonight.

Veronica enters R

'Morning, Veronica. Is he ready to meet his fate?

Veronica I think so. (*She goes quickly to the doorway of Pulman's office*) Are you ready for them?

Pulman Ready for anything.

Veronica (*to the mob*) Would you go in?

Eve We certainly will.

They all go in, including Veronica, who brings her pad and pencil

Pulman 'Morning, Eve. Peter. Rodney. Richard.

Eve (*sweetly*) 'Morning, Victim.

Pulman I thought we might distribute ourselves. Rather than sit round a table. One doesn't want the feeling of a conference. And today I am anything but in command.

Eve Bags me the ringside seat.

They all sit round below the desk area

Pulman You will have grasped the procedure. If one can call it a procedure. There are no rules.

Eve Anything goes?

Pulman Absolute freedom of speech. And may I assure you, with my hand where my heart used to be, that anything you say will be and will remain absolutely private.

Eve Pity. I was thinking of selling the film rights.

Pulman Veronica will record us, in shorthand, on her little pad. The record will be shown to you, to correct it if you think it needs correction. It will not be shown to the Chairman.

Spurling We believe you.

Pulman So. Here I stand, a human dartboard. I invite your slings, your arrows. I shall clutch your spears to my breast. Who wants to start?

Frame May I . . .? (*He stands*)

Pulman Of course.

Frame It's just that. I should explain, I do have this, I tried to get out of it, but absolutely vital, a project I have in mind, so I thought perhaps the best thing would be, since I have very little to say, but since I am after all, nominally at least, the A.D.P.R. person, perhaps if I could just, I don't mean give you a lead, but I have thought this thing through very carefully, naturally the question of criticizing one's, when one knows that the whole thing was meant for the, that extraordinary tycoon who, though one must reluctantly admire his, what shall we say, merchant adventurer know-how, one sees him selling glass beads to ignorant natives for a thousand per cent profit, but if only that can lead to his being a patron of the arts one might possibly forgive him, and David there, one's heart bleeds for him, having to deal with that appalling monster every day of his life, how anyone can possibly do it, but since someone must do it, if only to protect the rest of us from, I do believe that David does an absolutely marvellous job, God knows the problems he's got, God knows what he takes off our shoulders and on to his own, the thing is that this man, this Chairman is, let's put it as kindly as we can, he is a dreadful old-fashioned bully, what else can one say, Ducker put it perfectly, the whole style of paternalist autocrat, so outmoded, in the face of this David does a miraculous, I do think we should give him a total vote of, not confidence, he doesn't need our confidence, but total support and total loyalty, and thank God it's him not us that carries—this whole thing . . . (*With a last wave of his arms, he collapses*)

A silence

Richard I second that.

A silence

Eve I third that. If one can third.

Pulman I don't think we have motions. (*To Veronica*) Do we?

Veronica I don't think so.

Frame Would you forgive me now, David, terribly sorry, I must rush to this . . .

Pulman Of course. Thank you, Peter.

Frame (*generally*) And I do suggest that you—even if it's not a motion . . .

Frame goes, quickly, up the stairs R and off

Spurling Can we end the meeting there?

Pulman Is that everything?

Eve I thought it was marvellous, as far as it went. But not actually everything.

Pulman Eve? You?

Eve (*graciously yielding place*) Rodney.

Spurling I don't think I've got anything to say at all. Of any importance.

Pulman Of no importance?

Spurling You do your job. I do mine. Within limits. The limits are known, they're part of the job. If you don't accept the limits you don't accept the job. I do mine as well as I can. So do you. As far as I can see.

Eve It's only that if we're positively invited to discuss the Head of Department's failings . . .

Pulman As indeed you are.

Eve Would it not be a waste of a golden opportunity—Jesus, there's a double negative coming up—not to discuss his failings?

Pulman A shameful waste.

Eve Right. He's right.

Pulman Thank you, Eve.

Eve I mean, small failings. Like malversation.

Spurling Like what was that?

Eve I looked it up last night. "Corrupt behaviour in a position of trust or public office." I don't say malversation. I just say, like. Like for instance. Like for example. (*To Pulman*) Don't you think?

Veronica David isn't supposed to join in the discussion. To argue or anything.

Pulman Could I not argue but ask? Quite simply?

Veronica Yes, I should think you're allowed to do that.

Pulman Who is actually going to start? Not saying "like"—but criticizing?

Spurling Didn't I start? Just now?

Pulman It was judicious. Hardly critical.

Spurling If you want me to be critical . . .

Pulman It's what we're here for.

Spurling All right. Critical statement. I've worked for worse bosses.

Pulman Worse.

Spurling Yes.

Pulman And better?

Spurling All bosses tend to be worse than each other. Yes, one better. I thought. After him I was unemployed for a couple of years. So he was better but worse. Can I do a Peter Frame now, and leave? For a meeting or something? I really have nothing to say. As far as I know.

Pulman I don't think I can stop people coming and going. But I should like you to stay.

Spurling All right.

Pulman I may need you. (*Generally*) Can I hear some more voices from the floor? I was hoping you would have only too much to tell me.

Eve We are choosing our words. It takes time.

Pulman If it's any help—and I myself shan't speak, after this—when they did the criticism-upwards thing at United Tobacco, where it worked so well . . . they used labels. Adjectives or nouns. To define. Like "Bully". "Bureaucrat." "Slave-driver."

Eve Shall we think of something for you?

Pulman Do.

Eve Jesuit? Equivocator-General?

Pulman I knew you could do it.

Eve Master of Ambiguity? Doctor of Sophistry? Father of Lies?

Richard Forgive me, but aren't these all compliments?

Eve Are they?

Richard A Public Relations man who was not an accomplished liar would hardly rise in his profession.

Eve For instance Rodney?

Richard Rodney can't be said to have risen.

Eve Rodney's doing all right.

Richard Are you doing all right, Rodney?

Spurling Middling.

Richard An honest answer. Rodney is painfully handicapped by his lack of skill at equivocation. David is more fully equipped. As he should be, for his job.

Eve Granted, for the sake of argument, that Public Relations involves lying to the public . . .

Richard It involves recognizing the distinction between Truth and Image.

Eve That's right, lying to the public. Granted this. But do you think a good PR man should also, habitually, lie to his own staff?

Richard No. But does David?

Eve It's not the lying so much as the—what's the word I want? More than "unreliability", not so melodramatic as "treachery". Perfidiousness? You know, one hand shaking yours while the other throws the switch that opens the trapdoor that drops you into the cellar that converts you into meat pies . . . And he's smiling down at you. "Hullo! What are you doing down there?"

Richard David's never dropped me in anything.

Eve I'll say this for David though. He gives you what you think is an assurance—protection, support, I'll stand by you, nothing to fear. If you get back alive from the sausage-machine and re-read the assurance, you find some small print on the back which you hadn't read . . . And you hadn't realized that paragraph three can be interpreted in more than one way. (*To Richard*) That's why you're wrong to define David as a liar. (*To Veronica*) And the point is definition, isn't it? To make David see how we see him?

Veronica Yes, that's right.

Eve Not liar so much as swindler, double-dealer, con-man. The best short definition is "cheat".

A silence

Richard I didn't define David as a liar. Or as anything.

Pulman Would you care to?

Richard If you like.

Pulman If *you* like.

Richard I haven't got a ready-made word for you. The word that springs into my mind, simply as a starting-point, is integrity.

Eve You mean lack of?

Richard No, not at all. Lack of pretences. Lack of deception.

Eve Darling heart . . .

Richard I didn't say lack of guile. Of course he is infinitely guileful. And you know it. He doesn't deceive you on this point. He doesn't claim to be sincere. He doesn't claim to be anything he isn't. He demands that you should have a mind as subtle and as supple as his own. It's like doing *The Times* crossword puzzle with a constantly shifting set of clues. The puzzle is fiendishly difficult, but the nature of the problem is perfectly clear. Couldn't be clearer. David is a fully integrated man.

Eve (*to Veronica*) Can I criticize Richard some time? I long to.

Veronica No, that's not upwards.

Eve It certainly is not.

Veronica You can't do it if it's not upwards.

Eve Can I congratulate him?

Veronica Yes, I think you can do that.

Eve On his splendid demonstration of how to kiss the boss's arse and not be defiled?

Eve exits, angrily, up R

Spurling I think the meeting has come to an end . . .

Pulman Without Eve, who would have the heart to go on with it?

Spurling exits up R, *Pulman through the private door and up* L

Richard Listen. I was in a bad state. Terrible doubts.

Veronica About me? (*She starts replacing the chairs*)

Richard No, about me. I didn't know why I was doing what I was doing. I do now.

Veronica You do?

Richard I found out just now. Almost by accident. The word "integrity". Listen. The Organization—any organization like ours—is a direct and permanent assault—on our integrity as individuals.

Veronica And you found that out?

Richard Listen. The Organization wants us totally involved. Totally committed. Totally controlled. Totally in its power.

Veronica Yes.

Richard So it needs to know our minds. Because that's where control comes from. From knowing a man's mind, inside out. While he doesn't know yours.

Veronica Yes.

Richard The Organization has no right to know our minds. It has a right to demand work—good work—in the job we're doing. That is all. That is absolutely all.

Veronica I'm glad you've found out.

Richard When the Organization demands more than it should demand— from you as an individual—then you've got to fight. It's your duty. Fight for yourself as an individual. By concealing your mind. By lying. By cheating. By serving your own interests. Because the interests of the individual—any individual—are far more important than the interests of the Organization . . . And you knew all this already.

Veronica And now you do.

Richard I love you. I always did. I could never quite understand . . . I love you now, and I know why.

Veronica Good.

Richard kisses Veronica, as the Lights fade to a Black-out

SCENE 3

Veronica is working at her desk. Pulman is seated in his office. Richard enters it and goes to Pulman

Pulman Ah, Richard.

Richard Good morning, you wanted to see me.

Pulman Yes I've been such an unconscionable time about this, that I may seem rather absurdly out of date. But I simply wanted to ask, how are you, and are you enjoying yourself, and are we—the Department, the Organization—giving you what you want in life? You've been with us long enough now to give at least a provisional answer.

Richard Well, provisionally . . .

Pulman Of course. God knows, I won't hold you to it.

Richard I think the answer is yes. So far.

Pulman Do sit down.

Richard sits

My notion of running a Department is absurdly paternalistic. I want everyone to be happy. I try to give everyone what they want. The only problem is to know what they want.

Richard And to know that you're both using the same dictionary.

Pulman Yes. Very good.

Richard Thank you.

Pulman I sometimes wonder, do you ration your clever remarks? In order not to dazzle us too often?

Richard I'm simply trying to divert you from asking me what I want. Because I'm not sure of the answer, even provisionally.

Pulman With the others I know, pretty well. I've been with them longer. Rodney Spurling wants security. Eve wants amusement and excitement and admiration. Peter Frame—how shall I define what Peter wants?

Richard Large acts of creation?

Pulman Not bad. Oh, I have a monster screed from him. I think you've all had it.

Richard Yes, he was talking to me about it just now.

Pulman And did you respond with the required enthusiasm?

Richard I used my pondering technique.

Pulman No more than that?

Richard Perhaps a little more. I'm fond of Peter.

Pulman But?

Richard And it's a clever idea. I'd even say brilliant. Well thought-out. Well presented.

Pulman But?

Richard (*hesitating, then taking the plunge*) But fundamentally it's damn silly.

Pulman Ah.

Richard I take it you were asking for my opinion.

Pulman So how can I give Peter what he wants?

Richard Difficult.

Pulman Never mind, I'll think of something.

Richard I'm sure you will.

Pulman For you, I should have thought the provisional answer would have been "advancement".

Richard It did occur to me as a possible answer.

Pulman I once worked for an American who said five times a day, "I want all you fellas to be after my job".

Richard He was lying, of course.

Pulman Of course—I should quite like you to be after mine. After me. Don't say thank you, it'd be meaningless.

Richard Nevertheless.

Pulman Be myself, in my job, for a moment. What am I going to do about Peter?

Richard Console him with something else. He falls in love with a new idea very fast.

Pulman Yes, but before that. I do think we should give this idea a fair hearing first.

Richard Oh yes.

Pulman Democracy in action. It must not only be done but must be seen to be done.

Richard Yes, of course.

Pulman Now, let's see. Peter's screed has been circulated, we're going to discuss it this morning, we might even go so far as to vote on it. If we do, how will the voting go, d'you think? Myself abstaining, impartial in the chair . . .

Richard Peter in favour.

Pulman Only?

Richard Only.

Pulman Why do you think that?

Richard I don't see Rodney going along with such a conspicuously useless expenditure. And Eve thinks it's sillier than I do.

Pulman What worries me—if everyone has made up his mind already, can one possibly call that giving it a fair hearing?

Richard (*beginning to see the trap*) Well . . .

Pulman Do you think it might be fairer—at least, more apparently fair— if someone could help Peter present his case? Rather more calmly and dispassionately than Peter himself will do it? It needn't be someone who sincerely believes in the idea—better if he doesn't, and he argues the case simply as an intellectual exercise.

Richard Well, yes—I see your point . . .

Pulman I'd be most grateful.

Eve and Spurling enter up R *and come into Veronica's office*

Eve Hullo, Veronica. Go in yet?

Pulman comes to welcome them

Pulman Do come in.

Frame comes into Veronica's office

Spurling, Eve and Frame come into Pulman's office and sit around the desk as usual

Pulman (*sitting*) The agenda this morning is splendidly short, and we should be able to get through it in record time. There's only one thing to discuss. You've all had Peter's paper on his project for Greatrick to sponsor a symphony orchestra.

Eve His project.

Pulman Yes, didn't I say that?

Eve I mean, not "our project" or "the project".

Pulman His project.

Eve Thank you.

Pulman I gather that opinions may be rather divided on this. I myself shall sit sublimely above the conflict. Eve, I forbid you to question the word sublimely.

Eve The only possible adverb.

Pulman I thought so. Peter, they've all read it, but I'm sure there's something more you'd like to say. However briefly.

Frame (*standing*) Well, I won't repeat what I've said in my thing, reasoned arguments, I should just like to add, to inject a, what shall I say, personal note. I do rather tend to feel, let me put it like this, that perhaps the most valuable service I can render to the Department is not the day-to-day carrying on of what goes on in any case come hell or high water, but in deliberately sitting back—and throwing up—things, notions, projects—which are not, obviously not, in the mainstream of our normal activity, but which nevertheless may have a certain validity, may point the way to a new departure of some kind, may possibly lead to an expansion of the Department's activities, which perhaps, this is not meant as the slightest criticism, might not have occurred to anyone else, simply because you are all so totally involved, you have absolutely no time, what's the phrase, to stand and stare . . . And this project I'm putting up to you now, I think it must be taken not only for what it is, it could do a great deal for Greatrick, but also as an exemplar, a paradigm, of what may be expected from me in the future, in pursuance of what I take to be my major function, as a—if I can use the word without seeming—as a think-tank . . .

Pulman Thank you, Peter.

Frame (*exhausted*) Thank you . . . (*He sits*)

Pulman Who next? Richard?

Eve Why Richard?

Pulman Peter is asking for a verdict. At a court-martial the junior officer speaks first.

Eve Oh, are we court-martialling Peter?

Pulman We're trying his idea. The principle applies. Richard?

Richard (*standing*) My first reaction to Peter's paper was—forgive me, Peter——

Frame Of course.

Richard —was great admiration for the presentation—combined with strong doubts about the idea. I wanted time to ponder.

Frame Of course.

Richard I have now completely swung round to the other side.

Eve What other side?

Richard I now feel strong doubts—forgive me again—about the presentation. Combined with great admiration for the idea.

Pulman Explain, Richard.

Eve And make it good.

Pulman Eve, you will have your turn.

Richard Initial doubts about the idea: this Organization is completely philistine. The Chairman is a musical moron who doesn't know *God Save the Weasel* from *Pop Goes the Queen*.

Eve Now get out of that one.

Richard I agree, at first sight it seems ludicrous for us to sponsor any kind of orchestra.

Eve Stick to that word "ludicrous".

Richard This led me to consider the proper task of public relations. To reinforce the strong point—or the weak? To accentuate what is there already—or to compensate for what is not? So that the Organization, and the Chairman, have—or appear to have—no visible weakness?

Eve Richard, I know we said we'd play it deadpan, but don't you think you're overdoing it?

Richard Surely, what is weakest one must reinforce most strongly. The very fact that the Chairman thinks the *Air on the G String* is something to do with fan-dancers . . .

Eve Hey, that's my joke!

Richard Yes, thank you, Eve—makes it necessary for us to have a full orchestra, not just a quartet.

Frame Exactly. You're quite right. That's what I should have said.

Pulman Eve, your turn now?

Eve I know we're all half hypocrites. Do we have to be complete hypocrites?

Frame Eve, that's unfair . . .

Eve Oh yes, you too, darling. Except you're a sincere hypocrite, if there is such a thing, and there must be because I've just said it.

Richard You mean, Peter is sincere, but you don't agree with him?

Eve I mean, you can't fool all of the people all of the time. You can't have public relations as a complete sham. You've got to have a little bit of truth as the foundation for your lies.

Richard But how splendid to have our philistine Chairman supporting the arts. Spending some of his ill-gotten gains on a worthy cause.

Frame Hear, hear!

Richard However much it embarrasses Eve. (*He sits*)

Pulman Rodney? Sage and silent?

Eve Rodney, you're our honesty integrity boy. Give us a song, or show us your integrity.

Spurling (*to Frame*) What would it cost, quarter of a million a year?

Frame In the nature of.

Spurling Three things. I agree with Eve ...

Eve Thank you, Rodney.

Spurling As an exercise in public relations it's totally hypocritical.

Eve Right.

Spurling Secondly, I like symphony orchestras. I'm in favour of their being supported by whomever.

Eve Yes! But!

Spurling Thirdly, this kind of project is outside my area of judgement. (*To Pulman*) Are you going through the motions of a vote?

Pulman I think we should.

Spurling I abstain.

Pulman As the Chair does, too, of course. Those in favour are Peter and Richard. Those against?

Eve puts both hands up

What's the other one, Eve?

Eve The voice of common sense.

Pulman I don't think we can let him vote. It would create a dangerous precedent. Motion carried, two to one, two abstaining. Thank you, that's all. (*He rises*)

They all start going

Thank you, Eve, thank you, Richard. A pleasure to hear two opposing viewpoints so well put.

Spurling and Frame exit up R

Eve How much are viewpoints these days?

Eve exits through the private door and up L

Pulman gives Richard a smile and a helpless gesture, then sits at his desk. Richard goes to Veronica's office

Richard Trapped. By your bloody boss.

Veronica Your boss too.

Richard All right, my bloody boss.

Veronica He's terribly good at trapping people.

Richard He's great.

Veronica When they're the sort of people who can't resist the piece of cheese.

Richard Right.

Veronica What was the cheese?

Richard The prospect of advancement.

Veronica Ah yes. Clever.

Richard Dead clever.

Veronica (*rising*) Don't you want advancement?
Richard That is the piece of cheese I obviously can't resist.
Veronica So you want it. So have it.

He gazes at her for a time

Richard That's not it. The cheese in the trap is you. (*He pulls her to him*)
Veronica (*gazing back in his eyes*) That's nice. I like it.
Richard You are what I want.
Veronica Good.

Veronica and Richard kiss

> *Frame suddenly enters up* R *into Veronica's office on his way through to Pulman. He does not even notice Richard*

Frame Thing I forgot, I simply must say to David, won't take a moment...
(*He goes into Pulman's office*)

> *Richard smiles at Veronica and goes off up* R

David. Thing I forgot, I simply must say to you, won't take a moment.
Pulman Out with it.
Frame Well, to get the orchestra thing going, I do think we shall need a Steering Committee.
Pulman Of course. With yourself in the chair.
Frame Unless you...?
Pulman My dear Peter, it's your idea. Credit where credit is due.
Frame Thank you. Very good of you, David.
Pulman I think your Committee should be inter-departmental.
Frame Exactly. That's what I wanted to say. It's a prestige project, and consequently our responsibility, but of course anything that advertises the name of Greatrick, must be of interest to Advertising Department, and there are aspects, like a possible end-product, which are naturally the concern of Marketing and Sales.
Pulman And you may want, at some stage, to bring in people from Personnel and Finance.
Frame Very probably.
Pulman And formalize the whole thing.
Frame David, it might be the beginning of our take-over.
Pulman It might.
Frame Looking beyond. Beyond the orchestra.
Pulman It's a great idea, it won't be the only one you ever have.
Frame No, no.
Pulman I rather envisage... Can one have a Standing Steering Committee?
Frame For Special Projects.
Pulman Yes.
Frame Oh David, thank you. What a marvellous thought.

They shake hands

Pulman Logical progression, that's all.

Frame Yes.

Pulman But one thing does strike me. From now on. All this is going to be a hell of a lot of work.

Frame Yes. But tremendously exciting.

Pulman Yes. But a hell of a load. For you.

Frame Well, yes, you know me, I love it.

Pulman On top of everything you've got already. I just wondered, wanted to ask is there anything we can do to help?

Frame (*cogitating*) Well ...

Pulman All I have in mind is, you should be devoting yourself, every minute of the time, to whatever is most important.

A moment's silence, while Frame brings himself to say something

Frame Well—I'm very glad you brought this up, it's something I've had in my mind for, I haven't mentioned it before simply because, one never wants to seem to be avoiding any sort of, what, responsibility, but the whole thing of, rather because of Ken Grist being my predecessor, it was very much his kind of thing, the thing he was good at, but if I am really to devote myself to, and I do agree with you that I should, well, you know yourself, there are these—these minor administrative chores ...

Pulman (*deeply understanding*) Ah yes. Can we take anything off your shoulders there?

Frame They could perfectly well be done by—the person who would be perfect for it is Veronica, but I imagine she's far too busy—unless you ...

Pulman (*as if surprised*) Veronica? I'll see if I can manage it.

Frame If you think you might be able ...

Pulman I'll have to think about it.

Frame The duties are, mere matter of efficiency, capable girl like Veronica easily could ...

Pulman Yes, I'll see if I can spare her.

Frame It would be the most tremendous help.

Pulman Yes, well, I'll think about it.

Frame Thank you ...

Pulman Leave the door open, would you?

Frame Certainly ... Thank you, David ...

Frame goes through Veronica's office and off up R

(*As he passes Veronica*) I think he wants you ...

Veronica goes into Pulman's office

Veronica Do you want me?

Pulman Yes. Do you want a drink?

Veronica Why?

Pulman Why not?

Veronica You never do anything except for a reason.
Pulman Celebration.
Veronica Oh, whose?
Pulman Yours. Slightly more than mine.
Veronica What am I celebrating?

Pulman opens the desk drawer and takes out a handwritten draft memo, and gives it to Veronica. Then he goes to his drinks cabinet, opens it, and starts pouring two gin-and-tonics

Pulman Draft memo, you haven't seen it yet. You might like to type it, if you approve. Your last act as a secretary.
Veronica (*reading it*) Mmm.
Pulman I have the assurance of our friend the Head of Personnel that it will go through, as the French say, on wheels.
Veronica Money?
Pulman Mentioned there, lower down.
Veronica Ah yes.
Pulman I hate saying money out loud. It's so sacred.
Veronica "Administrative Assistant."
Pulman The best description I could think of. (*He brings her her drink*) Not congratulations, but thank you, and many happy returns. And cheers.
Veronica Cheers.
Pulman To your new life.
Veronica Can I ask . . . ?
Pulman Anything.
Veronica Peter is—out?
Pulman Sliding sideways, into Committee-land. But not gone yet.
Veronica But on the way?
Pulman The time will come when he storms in here and insists that I stop calling him "Assistant Director", he isn't Assistant Director at all, he's Special Projects.
Veronica Will the orchestra happen?
Pulman Whatever happens, there'll be this committee. There's nothing so permanent as the temporary.
Veronica Do you think it will happen?
Pulman I think probably. Do you?
Veronica I think two things.
Pulman Oh yes, what?
Veronica I think you got Peter to set up this inter-departmental thing, because the orchestra serves your purpose at the moment, but you don't really give a damn about it, but you do want to prove that you're not empire-building. Your hands are clean.
Pulman Clever girl.
Veronica I also think you stayed out of it yourself, because it'll break down sooner or later. Before it happens or after it happens—five years from now there'll be an economy wave—"Do we really need an orchestra?" And you can be detached and objective. "Yes, on the whole you're

right." You never even voted for the idea when it first came up. Your
hands are clean.

Pulman Clever me. How many birds with one stone?

Veronica Dozens.

Pulman Dozens.

Veronica I'm simply trying to prove I know where their bodies are
buried.

Pulman But of course you do.

Veronica I'm simply trying to prove—(*she indicates the draft memo*)—I
deserve more money than that, and a better title than that.

Pulman (*a bit taken aback*) Not polite blackmail?

Veronica No. I deserve it. That's all.

Pulman It would be difficult to push through.

Veronica I bet this one was terribly easy. You can do something a bit
more difficult.

Pulman It's possible. But advisable?

Veronica I should tell you, it's silly to keep these things a secret . . .

Pulman When they may have an effect . . .?

Veronica I have been rather associating with the other Departments
recently.

Pulman Discreetly, I'm sure.

Veronica Oh yes, they all want to know your secrets. They're jealous of
you because you have the ear of the Chairman.

Pulman The only part of him I want.

Veronica I have the definite offer of a better job, from Advertising. And
a terribly solid half-promise, from Marketing and Sales.

Pulman (*indicating the memo*) Better than . . .?

Veronica Yes.

Pulman Discuss money first? Or title?

Veronica Title first. Money follows. Don't you think?

Pulman Yes. "Administrative Assistant" seemed to me splendidly ac-
curate.

Veronica I hate "Assistant". It sounds like a jumped-up secretary.

Pulman Except "Assistant Director".

Veronica Which is hardly . . .

Pulman As yet . . .

Veronica As yet—"Assistant" first is all right. "Assistant" second is terrible.

Pulman What's up from Assistant?

Veronica Executive?

Pulman Veronica, darling, you are joking. And if you aren't, you must
be.

Veronica No.

Pulman "Administrative Executive", one can't even say it, it's a contradic-
tion in terms . . .

Veronica I read it in *The Times* the other day. Someone in some big firm.
"Administration Executive." I did. Really.

Pulman What monster have I bred?

Veronica Who bred me? Can I have another drink?

With a martyred air, Pulman goes towards the drinks cabinet with her glass, as the Lights fade to a Black-out

SCENE 4

Veronica is in her office. Eve comes in from the corridor up R *and down the stairs*

Eve Congratulations.
Veronica Thank you, Eve.
Eve What is it? Your new name?
Veronica Administration Executive.
Eve Wow! Who dreamed that one up?
Veronica Personnel, I suppose.
Eve It has its uses. New test for drunks. Stand on one leg and say "Administration Executive".
Veronica Nobody can.
Eve Well, I think it's great. Women should take over the Organization.
Veronica The only hope for it.
Eve Whose job are you going to take over next? A man's, I hope.
Veronica Eve, darling, I couldn't possibly do your job.
Eve Veronica, darling. The one great fact of life in an Organization—never admitted, never declared. Any first-class secretary—and you weren't just first-class, you were world champion—can do any executive's job, better than he can. She does it already, while he sits there being masculine and going out to lunch.
Veronica Yes. Oh, the masculine person in there wants to see you.
Eve Yes, what's it about?
Veronica I don't know, something he's got the wrong way round.
Eve I'll straighten him out. (*She goes into Pulman's office. There is no-one there*) Not here to be straightened. Pity.
Veronica He must have gone to the loo.
Eve You mean he goes to the loo, like other people? I thought he'd eliminated all human weaknesses.
Veronica He's working on it.
Eve The complete mechanical monster.

Pulman comes in by the private door

Pulman Eve—"monster" was one you didn't think of for the criticism session.

Veronica exits through her own door down R

Eve Pity.
Pulman Yes. Though you gave me enough to think about.

Eve That was the idea, wasn't it?

Pulman And I thought. That's not usual. Usually my mind darts about all over the place, it might be called thinking but it's the kind you use doing a jigsaw puzzle—oh look, there's a piece over there that fits, what about this piece over here . . . But what you said actually made me think. Consider. Consider myself, among other things. And I hadn't done that for years.

Eve Any result?

Pulman Yes, I came to a solemn conclusion. Solemn? You know me. I could never be totally solemn. But serious. Not quite laughing. Perhaps it's time, I said. It may be time.

Eve I like the cliffhanger element.

Pulman I thought you might.

Eve Time for what?

Pulman To consider the viability of my position here, as Head of this Department.

A slightly chill silence

Eve Cliffhanger still. What way consider it?

Pulman picks up some documents from his desk

Pulman Veronica's draft report of what was said at the session. She did it some time ago, I've been reading it. A number of times.

Eve Riveting, I should think.

Pulman Yes. (*He hands her a copy*) Copy for you. To correct, if she got anything wrong, or if there's anything you want to correct . . . You have my assurance, with no small print and no double meanings. It will not be shown to the Chairman. Or to anyone outside our own small though divided group.

Eve And? And then? I'm a child with a story-teller. And next?

Pulman My serious conclusion. If that is how some—even if only one— of my senior staff sees me, then I have not done a job here, and I ought to resign. (*He hands her a single sheet of paper*) Copy of my own draft, to the Chairman. Letter of resignation.

A silence

Eve (*partly in admiration*) You wicked bastard.

Pulman Eve, I shall correct it, and send it.

Eve Will you? No, sorry. Silly question, to you.

Pulman Eve, I cannot run a Department of which some members see me like that.

Eve Would it be an alternative solution for me to resign?

Pulman Eve, I'm too fond of you.

Eve Uh?

Pulman And you might have more difficulty than myself in finding other employment.

Eve Wouldn't it be a faster way of arriving at the same result?

Pulman Same result?

Eve You send in your resignation. The Chairman demands to know why.

Pulman I answer in general terms.

Eve When was the Chairman satisfied with an answer in general terms?

Pulman Of course, I can't guarantee what he will ask. Or what I shall have to answer.

Eve I can. And the result.

Pulman What?

Eve Same as if I resigned. Out.

Pulman What shall I say? You had your fun.

Eve And now I pay for it.

Pulman And now we stop joking . . .

A silence

Eve Would it be a solution if I rewrote this draft . . . ?

Pulman Corrected it?

Eve Corrected it.

Pulman It would be at the very least an interesting exercise in Public Relations.

Eve Making something mean the opposite.

Pulman Wouldn't it?

Eve holds the draft, then gives the copy of the resignation to Pulman

Eve I eat dirt. (*She goes to the door of Veronica's office*)

Pulman (*sweetly*) Eve, we all have to eat a peck of dirt before we die.

Eve goes into Veronica's office as Veronica enters it from down R. *They stare at each other for a moment, Eve holding the draft: then Eve turns and exits up* R

Veronica enters Pulman's office

Veronica That was quick work.

Pulman (*tearing up the letter*) Quicker than I thought. She really wants to hold on to her job.

Veronica Oh yes.

Pulman There was a very helpful line in Ducker's report. "The leader who varies his leadership behaviour will produce better performance." I have just varied my behaviour. I was a bully. Interesting.

Veronica And is that the end of the whole business of the criticism sessions?

Pulman For ever, I hope. (*He throws the letter in the wastepaper basket*)

Veronica Without your asking me how I see you?

Pulman Veronica—I didn't dare.

Veronica turns to her office as the Lights fade to a Black-out

SCENE 5

Frame is in Pulman's office with Pulman, who is being a bit boyishly charming and helpless

Frame David, you must make a decision.

Pulman My dear Peter, I think that everything you're saying is eminently sensible and practical. It's just that . . . Am I being a sentimentalist? But I'd rather not do it. I'd rather not even discuss it. So for my sake, may we please not even discuss it?

Frame David, you need an Assistant Director to help you.

Pulman I've got one. You.

Frame But I don't help you.

Pulman Nevertheless.

Frame David, you're being ridiculous.

Pulman But I like having you as Assistant Director. Whether you assist me or not.

Frame The point is, you need someone who can.

Pulman Do I?

Frame Obviously impossible for me, my whole time taken up, the Committee has proliferated . . .

Pulman Committees do.

Frame Do you know, we are bursting with ideas. We have half-a-dozen in the pipe-line, a study-group working on each . . . David, may I tell you something in absolute confidence?

Pulman Of course.

Frame I envisage the time when Special Projects becomes a Department in its own right.

Pulman Marvellous thought.

Frame I haven't said a word . . .

Pulman The thought is safe with me.

Frame Meanwhile continuing nominally under Public Relations——

Pulman —until the day . . .

Frame Exactly. But it does mean that you are lacking a strong right arm . . .

Pulman Amputee. I'm getting used to it.

Frame David. Since you insist on being so absurdly helpless about this. I must tell you, I have taken matters into my own hands.

Pulman Oh? How?

Frame I've talked to the Head of Personnel. He is perfectly prepared for me to move, how shall I put it, sideways. And for you to appoint someone else as Assistant Director of this Department.

Pulman My God. You're presenting me with a *fait accompli*.

Frame I am.

Pulman The first man who's done that to me for . . .

Frame The first time I've ever known you, to put it brutally, shilly-shally over a question like this.

Pulman I give way. Feebly. Since I have no choice.

Frame None.

Pulman A new strong right arm . . . Can I find one? Who?

Frame To my mind there is only one possible person. You will receive a memo from me shortly explaining the reasoning, the thought-processes that lie behind what may seem at first sight . . . In the meantime, I'll send Veronica in, and you will dictate a memo to the Head of Personnel.

Pulman If you say so.

Veronica enters her office from down R

Frame I do. (*He marches out to Veronica's office*) Veronica, David wants to dictate a memo.

Veronica Oh?

Frame While the iron is hot.

Frame exits up R

Veronica goes into Pulman's office

Pulman Veronica, you're not my secretary, nor anyone's secretary. You're an executive.

Veronica But you want me to take a memo. (*She picks up a pad and pencil which are lying handily on the desk*) For the last time.

Pulman It's very short. And very confidential.

Veronica Dictate.

Pulman Memo to Head of Personnel. Subject A.D.P.R. This is to confirm our agreement on changes within this Department which can now be put into effect, two dots and a dash. One. Frame to be re-titled Special Projects, capital S capital P. Salary scale unchanged. Two. The post of Assistant Director is now vacant. Appointment to be made.

Veronica End of message?

Pulman Mm.

Veronica You do choose the oddest way of telling me things.

Pulman Yes.

Veronica And making me wonder why.

Pulman The fun is in wondering why.

Veronica Whose fun? (*She starts to go*)

Pulman Veronica!

Veronica (*turning*) Yes?

Pulman Could you please arrange for me to see Rodney and Eve? Separately? As soon as they can?

Veronica Eve, you're having lunch with.

Pulman Ah yes. She can wait till then.

Veronica Rodney?

Pulman Please.

Veronica When does your new girl come?

Pulman It's your own fault, you've spoilt me for anyone else. God knows, these temporaries, these momentaries. We are not a home for illiterates. Nor are we a knocking-shop. At least I hope not.

Veronica goes to her own office

As Veronica reaches her room, Frame comes quickly down the stairs R *and rushes towards Pulman's office*

Frame (*as he passes her*) While the iron is hot.
Veronica What?

But he has already rushed past her into Pulman's office

Frame David. While the iron is hot. (*He has an envelope, which he thrusts into Pulman's hands*) My recommendation. And my reasons.

Veronica silently dials an internal number

Pulman Thank you, Peter. I look forward to reading them.
Frame Now, if I could just in a few words get your mind orientated in the right direction to receive my signals . . .
Pulman May I guess? You've recommended Richard.
Frame How did you know?
Pulman I followed your thought-processes. To their logical conclusion.
Frame Yes, logical, I'm so glad you agree.
Pulman The only person you would have recommended.
Frame Of course. The only. You're quite right. (*He goes out through Veronica's office, speaking to her as he passes*) Marvellous man. Never ceases to amaze me.

Frame exits up R

Veronica goes into Pulman's office

Veronica Rodney's just coming. How did you amaze Peter?
Pulman Shall I tell you something?
Veronica About Peter?
Pulman No. About you.
Veronica If you want to.
Pulman I have to appoint an Assistant Director.
Veronica I know that.
Pulman But who?

Veronica is silent

Veronica—if you were five years older, and not quite so deliciously pretty, and not quite so recently promoted to the ranks of the junior executives, I should be sorely tempted . . . No, that's the wrong word. I should be greatly tempted to offer the job to you.
Veronica It's nice of you to say so.
Pulman No.
Veronica At least, it's nice for me to know that you thought you ought to say so.
Pulman I do admire you. What a clever girl you are.
Veronica Yes.

Pulman And you understand.

Veronica Oh yes.

Pulman Seniority is boring but it exists. Richard is as young as I dare go.

Veronica I always assumed you would choose Richard.

Pulman He is equipped. He knows how to say the right thing at the right moment to the right person, how to wear the right face in the right place with the right people.

Veronica Public relations.

Pulman Human relations. The skills by which we manipulate others.

Veronica Have you told Richard you've chosen him?

Pulman Not yet. There are things I have to do first.

Veronica Oh?

Pulman I'm so glad. For your sake, too.

Veronica Why for my sake?

Pulman I suppose I'm a romantic.

Veronica gives him a look of amused disbelief and turns back to her own office

Rodney comes down the stairs R

Spurling Hullo, Veronica.

Veronica Hullo, Rodney.

Spurling David wanted to see me.

Veronica The last romantic.

Pulman (*coming to the doorway*) Oh Rodney, do go in. Veronica, have you got that memo?

Veronica Coming. (*She finishes typing it*)

Pulman and Spurling go into Spurling's office

Pulman Drink, Rodney?

Spurling No, thanks.

Pulman Nor me, then. A moderate man in my own belief, I start finding the mornings and afternoons are longer. I think drink-time comes before it does. Age, I suppose. Or the Chairman.

Spurling Or both.

Pulman Mm. Do sit down.

Spurling (*not sitting*) Been sitting all morning.

Veronica comes in with the memo

Veronica The memo. (*She gives it to Pulman and goes out again, to sit at her desk*)

Pulman You my oldest, and triedest, and truest . . .

Spurling I can still stand. Just.

Pulman I want to show you something. Confidential, of course. Hence the offer of a drink. I never understand the connection between confidentiality and alcohol, but there seems to be one. (*He gives the memo to Spurling*) Copy of my memo to the Head of Personnel.

Spurling (*reading it*) Mm.

Pulman Splendidly non-committal reaction.
Spurling One could see it coming. Now it's come.
Pulman Yes. There is a vacancy. For a quite important job. Seemingly
important, at least. The title resounds with a certain clangour.
Spurling A hollow clangour. (*He hands Pulman the memo*)
Pulman We know that. Not everyone does.
Spurling Mm.
Pulman Always a mistake to announce a vacancy. It leads to everything
we don't want here. Speculation, rivalry, intrigue.
Spurling You'd better appoint someone.
Pulman Always a mistake to keep a vacancy vacant. Or some clever chap
like the Chairman will say, "You don't need one. Abolish the post."
Spurling Do you in fact need one?
Pulman In fact, no.
Spurling Abolish the post.
Pulman What? And be the one and only departmental head with no
Assistant Director? My reputation would never recover.
Spurling Prestige is all.
Pulman Almost all. I must appoint someone to this totally unnecessary
job. And make a double announcement. New A.D.P.R.—and Peter
Frame as Special Projects.
Spurling So . . .?
Pulman You are our senior and most-respected member. It would mean
slightly more money, not much but slightly. The choice is obvious. I
am offering you the job.
Spurling The totally unnecessary job.
Pulman (*with his charming smile*) Yes.

A silence

Spurling Would you like me to turn it down straight away? Or pretend
to think about it overnight?
Pulman I'd like you to accept.

A silence

Spurling Everybody here clings to some fallacious conviction about him-
self. It's a sort of psychological device we use, to reconcile ourselves
to being here. My own fallacious conviction is that I am expert in my
present job.
Pulman Not fallacious at all. You are.
Spurling A conviction. From which it follows that in any other job I'd be
less expert.
Pulman That may or may not be true.
Spurling In an unnecessary job, I'd be conspicuously unnecessary.
Pulman I don't think so, Rodney.
Spurling Forgive me. It's my conviction.
Pulman As you say.
Spurling Besides, you can do better than me.
Pulman Oh, who?

Spurling Richard.
Pulman Richard? Why do you say that?
Spurling I'll send you a memo.

Eve enters up R *and comes down the stairs. Spurling exits through the private door and up* L

Eve Hi.
Veronica Hullo, Eve, you come for lunch?
Eve Yes, what is it, a peace-offering? (*She goes on into Pulman's office*) 'Morning, boss. Ready for lunch?
Pulman Thank you for accepting at such short notice.
Eve Ever ready.
Pulman Today I am light-hearted. Frivolous. I suddenly thought, I don't want a lunch discussing business. I want pure pleasure. A meal with a beautiful, charming, amusing woman.
Eve Me.
Pulman Yes.
Eve Beautiful, charming, amusing woman from the office.
Pulman As it happens.
Eve But pure pleasure.
Pulman Unalloyed.
Eve Good word.
Pulman I want, metaphorically speaking, to put my feet up on you.
Eve You mean, you're not going to start talking business until we've got to the second cup of coffee?
Pulman Rather do it now? Get it over with?
Eve Yes.
Pulman Might spoil your appetite.
Eve Chance it.
Pulman Hm. Well. Where to start.
Eve Shall I start you?
Pulman Please.
Eve Once upon a time, there was a dear departed dumb-bell called Ken Grist.
Pulman Yes, there was.
Eve Who happened, through no fault of his own, to be your Assistant Director.
Pulman Yes, he was.
Eve He was so notoriously useless, he got fired, and his job was given to Peter Frame.
Pulman Yes, it was.
Eve Peter wasn't stupid, but he was mad. So you shunted him off into a siding called Special Projects.
Pulman You might put it like that.
Eve You are the kind of Head of Department, and there's only one kind, which is you . . . who needs a second in command, hardworking but not a rival. Not a danger. Not a threat.
Pulman If you say so.

Eve Ken wasn't, because he was a moron, Peter wasn't, because he's a maniac. Richard isn't, because he's too young.

Pulman Isn't youth an advantage these days?

Eve You are going to appoint Richard as Assistant Director, but first of all you have to square two old lags: Rodney, and me. Have you squared Rodney yet?

Pulman I offered it to Rodney.

Eve Offered it?

Pulman The thing. The post. A.D.P.R. Just now.

Eve In what terms, on what conditions?

Pulman I simply offered it.

Eve Simply?

Pulman He turned it down.

Eve Clever David.

Pulman So now I'm offering it to you.

Eve What?

Pulman The thing. The post. A.D.P.R. Would you care to accept? Then we'll go and have lunch.

A pause

Eve Yes. I accept.

Pulman Good. Great. Out. Lunch.

Eve But.

Pulman I have no buts.

Eve But with me, you're going to make conditions.

Pulman No.

Eve None?

Pulman The only condition is, that you perform the duties of A.D.P.R.

Eve Which are?

Pulman You know what they are.

Eve Tell me.

Pulman To be—what's that dreadful expression? To be my strong right arm. Faithfully. Loyally. Devotedly.

She looks at him

Eve Can I have lunch? A very big, expensive lunch? . . . Instead?

Pulman makes a gesture of reluctant acceptance

Eve and Pulman go out through the private door and by the lift L. Richard appears in the corridor R and watches them go, then goes down into Veronica's office

Richard They've gone.

Veronica Good. (*Rising*) Shall we?

Richard Come and have an impossibly expensive lunch. I want to reduce my bank account to zero, at one fell swoop.

Veronica You want to be poor?

Richard I want you to love me for myself alone. I want to come to you empty-handed.

Veronica Risk. I might not like empty hands.
Richard It's simpler. Start with nothing. Start clean.
Veronica Yes. Simpler.
Richard I want to marry you. I want you to marry me. Whichever way round it is. I want us to live together, legally. Again, it's simpler . . . I love you.
Veronica Yes. I love you. I think.

They embrace

Richard You think . . . ?

They part

Veronica I'm fairly sure I do, most of the time.
Richard Most of the time you're sure? Or just fairly sure?
Veronica Fairly sure.
Richard Jesus.
Veronica Most evenings I'm sure. No, not in the office, I hate office *affaires*.
Richard We're not an office *affaire*.
Veronica Aren't we?
Richard I love you. That's all.
Veronica Not all. It can't be.
Richard I'd have fallen in love with you whenever wherever I met you. The office is just the place I happened to meet you.
Veronica I can feel David's eye on us. "Oh look, those two are in love. I can use that. How shall I use it?"
Richard He can't use it.
Veronica Oh yes he will. It's called human relations.
Richard Stick to what's important.
Veronica The important thing is, what are you going to do in life?
Richard You inquiring about my prospects?
Veronica No. Just what are you going to do?
Richard Earn a living. Enjoy myself. With you, I hope.
Veronica I don't want to marry a eunuch.
Richard You wait. I'll give you eunuch.
Veronica One of the first things I ever said to you was, "In the old days the Chairman used to cut their balls off personally".
Richard I remember. I thought you were a funny lady. Not just a pretty face.
Veronica It was more of a warning.
Richard I got that, too.
Veronica I should have said, "These days they melt them off. Without your noticing."
Richard You mean me?
Veronica I mean there are two ways you can end up. A successful adjusted eunuch like David. Or a failed neurotic eunuch like most of the others.
Richard In either case . . . ?
Veronica Have you met any who aren't? After the first year or two? It happens to them. To all of them.
Richard Would you marry me if I left the Organization?

Veronica Yes. The next day.

Richard tears the top piece of paper off the pad and exits up R as the Lights fade to a Black-out

SCENE 6

Veronica is in her office. Pulman enters from the lift L and goes along the corridor into her office

Pulman Veronica, since we have no secrets from each other . . .
Veronica Really?
Pulman In the sense that you can read me like a book.
Veronica Sometimes the print is a bit small.
Pulman Never for your eyes. Will you help me to read someone else? Where the print is so small, I can't at the moment decipher it?
Veronica Who?
Pulman Richard. I am failing to follow his mood.
Veronica Oh?
Pulman Usually, of course, I don't follow, I lead. He follows, with the utmost skill. He stops joking at exactly the same moment as I do. Whereas Eve, darling woman, such a natural person, goes on joking just that moment too long.
Veronica The skills of being a subordinate.
Pulman The skills of being a subordinate who seeks advancement. As Richard does.
Veronica Does he?
Pulman I thought so, till now.
Veronica But now . . . ?
Pulman I am puzzled by his mood. Moods, in the plural. He seems to swing from the farouche to the mystically exalted. As if he were about to turn monk, or climb Everest.
Veronica Everest perhaps. I don't think monk.
Pulman Some sort of crisis, deep in his soul.
Veronica Have you told Richard you're going to appoint him A.D.P.R.?
Pulman No more than a half-indication. Deliberately vague.
Veronica You'll have to tell him sooner or later. He can't become Assistant Director without knowing.
Pulman I suppose not. Veronica, you are not going to stand in his way?
Veronica No.
Pulman I'm glad. I shouldn't like you to stand in his way.
Veronica I am not going to stand in his way.

Frame enters up R at an agitated run, comes down to Veronica's office and takes Pulman into Pulman's office

Frame David! . . . David! . . . I must speak to you in your office. Excuse us, Veronica. David, the most extraordinary thing.

Pulman What?

Veronica sits at her desk with her head in her hands

Frame It's Richard. He's in his office, reciting something at the top of his voice, and screaming with laughter like a maniac!

Pulman (*still calm*) Well, well.

Frame I heard him—I couldn't help hearing him. What do you think we ought to do?

Pulman I think we should wait.

Frame Wait? For what?

Pulman For what happens next.

Frame Of course. Absolutely right.

Richard comes along quickly up R and comes in at Veronica's office. He is not obviously mad, but his manner is somewhat peculiar. He enters Pulman's office

Pulman Good morning, Richard. How well-timed. I was just going to ask you to come.

Richard (*presenting an envelope*) I brought a message.

Pulman (*taking it*) For me?

Richard Yes.

Pulman From . . .?

Richard Me.

Pulman Thank you. So much safer than the internal mail. (*He drops it on his desk*)

Richard I'd like you to read it.

Pulman And I shall.

Richard I'd like you to read it now. Or shall I read it to you?

Pulman I'm afraid it must take second place to more immediate business.

Frame David—Richard—would you excuse me, are you going to . . .?

Pulman Of course.

Frame Yes. I entirely agree. (*To Richard*) Congratulations. (*To Pulman*) I'll tell the others. (*To Richard*) Well done, Richard.

Frame rushes through Veronica's office and out up R

A silence

Richard Tell the others what?

Pulman I now feel the confidence to offer you the post of Assistant Director, Public Relations, the Greatrick Organization, which I have been wanting to offer you for some time. You'll start at the lower end of the salary scale, of course. But even the lower end is a considerable advance.

Richard No . . .

Pulman No, question mark? Or no, exclamation mark?

Richard I can't. You can't.

Pulman Richard, may I tell you two things? I always say that, and then I can't think of two, or I find there are three things. However . . . Do sit down.

Richard sits

Firstly. A man must not deny his natural talents. You are intelligent, hardworking, ambitious but not outrageously so, co-operative—better than co-operative. You have the greatest quality of all: you are flexible.

Richard Too goddamn flexible.

Pulman I didn't say pliable. Big difference. Flexible.

Richard So you're offering me the job.

Pulman You have this marvellous talent. With an eager smile on your face, and with equal sincerity, you can run with the hare and hunt with the hounds.

Richard Christ.

Pulman Secondly. People of normal sensitivity who join an Organization like this—as I did once—go through some kind of crisis, within a year or so. Most recover—as I hope you are on the road to recovery. Those who don't, rush off and join some other Organization. And when they get there they find that the colour of the walls is different. But the Organization isn't other. It's the same.

Richard Yes, I believe that.

Pulman What they tried to run away from is the normal destiny of mankind.

Richard Yes, I accept that.

Pulman I urge you to accept my offer.

Richard May I think about it?

Pulman No, exclamation mark. It's been thought about long enough. You can have one minute . . . Oh, there is a thirdly. You are recommended for the job by Peter Frame, and Rodney Spurling, and Eve.

Richard Am I?

Pulman Separately, individually, in private, to me. Unanimous. Want to ring them and check?

Richard (*on the road to recovery*) I apologize for being so—*farouche* . . .

Pulman Not at all. We've all been through it, in our time.

Richard And apologize for my hesitation.

Pulman Natural modesty.

Richard May I ask?

Pulman Anything.

Richard Am I—your idea? Have I you to thank . . .?

Pulman Don't thank me, I serve no-one's purposes but my own.

Richard And Veronica . . .?

Pulman Nothing has been hidden from Veronica. Nothing ever is.

Richard (*agreeing*) No.

Pulman She always assumed you would get the job. She knew for certain it was you—what, a couple of days ago?

Richard Did she?

Pulman What a perfectly splendid girl she is. She behaved really remarkably well—not standing in your way—considering that she was your one and only rival for the job.

A silence

Richard I accept.
Pulman Good. Splendid.

Pulman holds his hand out. They shake. Richard starts to go. Pulman picks up Richard's letter from the desk

Pulman I imagine that the message is now out of date?
Richard (*taking it*) There's one or two things in it I'd like to rewrite.
Pulman I look forward to reading it.
Richard (*with boyish charm*) I think you'll enjoy it. Would you forgive me. I just . . .
Pulman No, no. (*He goes to the door to Veronica's office and beckons her in*)

Veronica enters Pulman's office. Pulman sits on the corner of the desk in Veronica's office, facing upstage

Richard Why didn't you tell me?
Veronica Tell you what?
Richard You were after the job.
Veronica Did you accept it?
Richard Yes.
Veronica Then it doesn't matter.
Richard But why didn't you tell me?
Veronica It doesn't matter.
Richard Is that why you wanted me to leave?
Veronica No.
Richard Then what reason?
Veronica I wanted you to leave because I wanted you to leave.
Richard And you'd have a clear field.
Veronica No!
Richard You would have had.
Veronica Did David say that?
Richard He thought you'd been perfectly splendid—not standing in my way. He didn't know.
Veronica There's nothing he doesn't know.
Richard Do you deny it? That you tried to make me leave?
Veronica I wanted you to leave because it was your one chance of saving your soul.
Richard Oh?
Veronica I wanted you to leave by saying you were leaving, and leaving. Doing it straight. Of your own accord. Just like that.

A silence

Is that your letter of resignation?
Richard Yes.
Veronica Can I see it? Just for fun?

He hands her the letter. She opens it and reads it, amused by it

Was this what you were reading out loud—and laughing?
Richard Yes . . .

Veronica It's good stuff—funny.
Richard I could send it.
Veronica (*not challengingly*) But you won't.
Richard (*not defiantly*) No, I won't.

Eve, Frame and Spurling enter up R and come down into Veronica's office

Spurling goes to the doorway to Pulman's office, checks inside, then beckons them all in. They follow him, and he goes over to the drinks cabinet where he prepares bottles and glasses ready for a party

Pulman Ah. Champagne.
All Congratulations, Richard.
Eve And the first time I set eyes on you, I said, "That man is an Assistant Director".
Richard (*all charm*) What made you say that?
Eve Boyish charm. Concealing guile. Concealing frankness. Concealing guile. Concealing integrity. Concealing guile.
Richard Eve, so perceptive.
Eve I know an onion when I see one.
Spurling Congratulations, onion.
Richard Thank you, Rodney.
Spurling Seek refuge in domestic happiness. If you can find it.
Richard I hope to find it.
Spurling It's a hope.
Frame And if you can help talk the Chairman into being a patron of the arts . . .
Richard I gather he's a bit difficult.
Frame But you're so brilliant at persuading people to do what they never intended to do . . .
Veronica (*passing*) Starting with himself.
Frame Oh, why d'you say that?
Veronica No reason.

Veronica moves away. Richard follows

Richard Veronica, did you want the job?
Veronica I could have handled it.
Richard I can't? I still love you.
Veronica Administration Executives do not associate with Assistant Directors. Except at work.
Richard Before work? After work?
Veronica Work's work. It wouldn't work.

Pulman comes up with a bottle of champagne

Pulman Richard. Drink. Your party.
Richard Lovely party.
All Well done, Richard.
Pulman Veronica?

Veronica No, thank you.

Pulman You wouldn't want us to think you weren't celebrating.

Veronica I sometimes wish I worked for an old-fashioned bully.

Pulman I do. You wouldn't like it.

Veronica You're a tyrant.

Pulman Under-tyrant. Sub-tyrant.

Veronica Modern tyrant. Manipulating people. The real tyranny. (*She moves away into her own office, and stands up beside the coffee-vending machine*)

Pulman Veronica being difficult?

Richard You do know I want to marry her.

Pulman My dear fellow. With your constantly developing skills . . . you should be able to talk her into it. Anyway, it'll be marvellous practice.

The party goes on, very cheerfully. The Lights fade to two spots, one on Richard and one on Veronica. The spot on Veronica fades; then the one on Richard, as—

the CURTAIN *falls*

FURNITURE AND PROPERTY LIST

NOTE: To shorten the Black-outs as much as possible, the few props required for each following scene should, where practicable, be brought on or struck by members of the cast

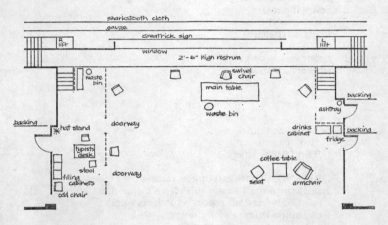

ACT I

MAIN OFFICE

On stage: Large desk. *On it:* desk set and tidy, blotter, pens and pencils, ashtrays, memo paper, 2 telephones, intercom (practical)

Large executive swivel chair

5 leather office chairs

Low coffee table. *On it:* ashtray, telephone, magazines

Armchair

Matching seat

Drinks cabinet. *On it:* tray of glasses, bottles, glass decanter. *In it:* champagne glasses, sherry glasses, assorted drinks, splits

Refrigerator. *On it:* ice bucket, pot plant. *In it:* ice cubes

Waste bin under desk

Floor-standing ashtray

SECRETARY'S OFFICE

Typist's desk. *On it:* electric typewriter (practical), 2 telephones, intercom (practical), mini switchboard, assorted papers, pencils, pens, pads, books, etc.

Multi-drawer filing cabinet

2 two-drawer filing cabinets. *In them:* 2 special magazines (Bulletin and House), various office files

Coffee-vending machine (practical) with paper cups

Hat/coat stand. *In it:* umbrella

Chair

Low stool

2 waste bins—one under coffee machine
Across large window at back of corridor: large sign GREATRICK in
   reverse lettering
Floor and corridor carpets

Off stage: Carton with bottles of gin, whisky, tonic water, ginger ale **(Veronica)**
   Tray with coffee pot, 2 cups, saucers and spoons, cream jug, sugar bowl
     (Veronica)
   Script **(Richard)**
   Script **(Frame)**
   2 suitcases **(Pulman)**
   Briefcase **(Pulman)**

Personal: **Grist:** watch, coins
   Ducker: notebook

ACT II

Strike: Suitcases and other cases
   "Used" papers
   GREATRICK lettering

Set: ORGANIZATION lettering in reverse on window
   Handwritten draft memo in **Pulman's** desk drawer
   Copies of typed draft report on **Pulman's** desk
   Resignation letter in desk drawer
   Pad and pencil on **Pulman's** desk
   Champagne bottles in drinks cabinet

Off stage: Resignation letter in envelope **(Frame)**
   Resignation letter in envelope **(Richard)**

LIGHTING PLOT

Property fittings required: modern office wall fittings
Interior. Offices. The same scene throughout

ACT I

ACT II

Cue 16	**Veronica:** "Can I have another drink?" *Fade to Black-out*	(Page 58)
Cue 17	When ready *Bring up to day lighting*	(Page 58)
Cue 18	**Pulman:** "Veronica—I didn't dare." *Fade to Black-out*	(Page 60)
Cue 19	When ready *Bring up to day lighting*	(Page 60)
Cue 20	**Veronica:** "The next day." *Fade to Black-out*	(Page 69)
Cue 21	When ready *Bring up to day lighting*	(Page 69)
Cue 22	**Pulman:** ". . . it'll be marvellous practice." *Pause, then fade to spot on* **Veronica** *and spot on* **Richard** *Fade spot on* **Veronica,** *then spot on* **Richard,** *to Black-out* *for* CURTAIN	(Page 74)

EFFECTS PLOT

ACT I

ACT II

No cues